D1156304

Christ in Our World

This book is dedicated to
our Mother the Church

Contents

Preface

ONE OF THE most urgent needs of our day, one deeply reflected in the debates at Vatican II, is that of theological *relevance*. Books such as *Honest to God* and the cry on the part of some theologians that "God is dead" bear testimony to this urgent need. For God does live, but theologians have been singularly inept in disclosing to contemporary man that the God of whom they speak is a living, personal being, engaged in human history and efficaciously present to his people.

It is for this reason that *Christ in Our World* is an important, stirring book, for in it two leading British theologians, one a well-known biblical scholar and the other an expert in modern catechetical developments, attempt to show that the God of Christians is a living God who makes himself known through history, through the ordinary events of human life, that he is truly one with his people. Through history the living God has revealed that he is triune, and the culminating event in history is God's irruption into human events in the person of Jesus Christ, through whom and in whom the Father is revealed and who now dwells in the midst of the people he has chosen through the Spirit sent jointly by the Father and the Son.

Fathers Richards and De Rosa achieve their goal by centering attention on the dynamism of the sacraments which flow from the primordial sacrament, Christ, into the life of the people of the Church. Father Richards provides the historical and biblical background necessary if we are to grasp the root meaning of the sacraments as acts of Christ, searching the scriptures to dig out the rich depth of theological and existential significance of the sacraments rooted in the Christ of the New

Testament. Father De Rosa focuses attention on the meaning of the sacraments *today*, as efficacious and vital signs within the Church of Christ's abiding presence. In commenting on the meaning of the sacraments today, Father De Rosa likewise has some penetrating observations to make regarding actual practice, and his suggestions for making sacramental worship more meaningful will be welcomed by everyone.

The need to make our religious faith relevant to modern man is indeed well served by the authors of this stimulating volume. Their work will be of immense value to the mass of Christian people seeking to bring themselves in line with the currents of thought sweeping the Church today. Pastors and all concerned with religious education will find it an exceptionally worthwhile sourcebook.

William May

Foreword

THE KIND RECEPTION given to these lectures when they were first delivered has encouraged us to seek for a wider public by publishing them now. We are well aware of the hazards in doing this.

Firstly, there is a marked difference of style between the two of us; and, secondly, the ways of speaking scarcely coincide today with the ways of writing. We have done our best to make the material and its presentation as harmonious as we could. Needless to say, there remain many deficiencies we would like to have eliminated had there been time, that most precious and elusive of commodities, available. But with new work pressing hard upon us we knew that no further opportunities were likely to present themselves for improving a book which we had to decide either to print in this imperfect form or never to print at all. It is for the reader to make up his mind which would have proved the wiser course.

We would like to thank Father Nigel Larn for inviting us to give the lectures at Hopwood Hall, so enabling us to participate in a week whose success was guaranteed by his own enthusiasm and extraordinary talent for organization.

Our gratitude is also due to his Lordship the Bishop of Galloway. He has not only contributed the Preface to this book: his presence at all the lectures was an inspiration to everyone.

It remains to say that the chapters with "Scripture" in the title were written by Father H. J. Richards, those with "World" in the title by Father Peter De Rosa.

3 October, 1965

Corpus Christi College,
17–23 Denbigh Road,
Bayswater,
London W.11

I

THE CHURCH IN THE WORLD TODAY

THE TITLE OF THIS initial chapter has a rather grandiose air about it. Not only does it seem to credit its author with a kind of encyclopaedic knowledge of the contemporary world which he does not possess; it may also give the impression that the Church has, in our day, a role to play which she has not played in previous ages. That is false. She has but one role to play in all ages: to bring men to Christ, or better, to bring Christ to men. In every age to proclaim Christ and nothing but Christ.

A young woman who had studied in Paris once remarked that when she began reading the works of François Mauriac she found him so Christ-centred she thought he was a Protestant. How serious a criticism it would be if the Church were not completely and manifestly Christ-centred. That so many of us Catholics do not imitate better Mother Church in her Christ-centredness is probably the main reason why we find St Paul a little too Protestant for comfort.

It might almost be said that the main ecumenical task facing Catholics today is to convince our fellow Christians that Christ really is the root and foundation of the Catholic Church, that we do truly believe in, and act towards Christ as the one Mediator between God and men. This sounds easy enough to do in theory. In fact, it is extraordinarily difficult. To be able to achieve it we would have to become much more worthy of the Lord than we are. We would need to reflect more deeply than we are accustomed to do, as deeply as Paul VI encouraged us to do in his encyclical *Ecclesiam Suam*, on the nature of the

1

Church herself. "The first benefit," he wrote, "which we trust the Church will reap from a deepened self-awareness, is a renewed discovery of its vital bond of union with Christ. This is something which is perfectly well known, but it is supremely important and absolutely essential. It can never be sufficiently understood, meditated upon and preached" (§35).

The Church is so close to Christ as to be worthy to be called his bride whom Christ loves as his own body, as his own flesh and blood. And the bride seeks for nothing but to praise and to proclaim to the nations her husband and lord; and to share his life with the world of today and every day. Nothing must obscure this witness, no frills, no trimmings must be allowed to do so. Nothing must hinder the Church's channelling of his life. In her, says Origen referring to the Church, is the whole coming of the Son of God. She is full of the Trinity.

We can speak of the Church, built as she is in the image of Christ's Mother Mary, words which Dante put upon the lips of St Bernard as he ushers the soul into the divine presence. Indicating the Virgin he says: "Look now upon the face that most resembles Christ's, for the beauty of that face can alone prepare thee to see the face of Christ."

The beauty of the Church's face, even in the days of her pilgrimage, is a beauty mirroring the beauty of Christ's face. Her union with her Lord is, to quote Pope Paul once more, "the principal item, surely, of the whole of our religious heritage". Men should be able to look at her and say: "Now I know what Christ is like"—just as we can look at Christ and say: "Now I know what God is like."

The Church best shows what Christ is like in her sacraments. All the graces she bestows are christenings, a fashioning of men into the likeness of Jesus crucified and risen. Not an external fashioning, this, and the likeness is of love.

The Church has christened—or endeavoured to—all men in all the ages. Essentially her purposes remain the same, or rather her purpose, for she has but one: to bring about a union between men and God through the one Mediator Christ, in oneness with the Holy Spirit.

The infinity of man

But as one set of fingerprints differs from another, so there is a rich variation in each of the times and seasons of history. Man is made in the image of God. He, too, is "an infinite" struggling with the burden and promise of his own spirituality.

What is meant by spirituality? Dr Frank Sheed tells the story of his own attempt to explain what it is to a group of people in Hyde Park. The soul, he was declaiming, has no weight, no size or dimensions, no colour, etc. At this moment, a wag in the crowd stopped him short in the tracks of his eloquence with: "That's the best definition of nothing I ever heard."

The wag had a point. Man's spirituality—or, to use a concrete term, man's soul—is defined not in terms of nothing but in terms of everything. St Thomas Aquinas never tired of repeating Aristotle's dictum: "The soul is, in a sense, everything."

Man, by reason of his spirituality, is capable of establishing relationships with everything there is, including God who is the first source of everything.

This is why man is a paradox upon the earth. Part of nature, he is at birth the weakest thing there is. But because of his reason he is above nature. Nature brought him forth but cannot cope with him or cater for him. To animals, nature gives teeth and claws and a thick hide to keep out the cold. They are well provided for. Man, by contrast, is a gummy, clawless, naked bundle of soft flesh.

Is this unfair of nature? Is it improvident of God? It may seem so at first but it is not. Nature—or God by means of nature—*cannot* provide for man. Man is above nature, mightier than his mother. She cannot supply him with instincts to cater for his needs, for his needs are endless. This is why he is ever inventive, the ever-insatiable.

The wren will build its nest, the spider its web, from millenium to millenium in unchanging ways. But man sadly and gloriously is never still. Not satisfied with houses to live in, he required churches to worship in, and he builds them not in one style but in many—Anglo-Saxon, Norman, Gothic, Romanesque, Byzantine.

Nature works in fixed patterns in the animal kingdom, with the incidental variations due to biological evolution. Man, however, is a bird with not one but a million songs. As a social being he evolves more new patterns of living in half a year than the whole of nature in twenty million centuries. His mind, like his desires, knows no boundaries: it is in no sense a cul-de-sac but is ever open. It has an infinite plasticity about it and all the findings are pooled and transmitted socially.

So man escapes to a large extent from organic thraldom. Because his mind is open his hands are never still, those hands which Aristotle called the instrument of instruments, the tool of tools.

The Church, true Mother of men

The Church cannot ignore or fail to sympathize with this restlessness of man. She is called upon to favour it, to sanctify its products when they are good. She must have the discernment to distinguish between them.

If man were an animal pure and simple, the Church could have a ready-made formula to make him holy—same nest for the wren, same web for the spider, same ritualism and formulae for man.

But man cannot be catered for at one fell swoop by the Church any more than by nature. He is too volatile, too versatile, too dynamic a thing for that. However, the Church unlike nature is not blind; and she is not less mighty than man but mightier. She is his true Mother. She brought him forth to a life higher even than that of reason which nature did not give him. She understands him. She holds the secret of his existence. She has the truth which will sate his mind, the life which can fulfil his desires. In her, we said, is the whole coming of the Son of God—and he, Christ, is truth and life.

In Christ, God has told us all he knows, he has given us all the life we shall ever possess. But—and this too we have said already—the Church needs to bring Christ to men, to all generations of men, to human beings as they now are at their particular stage of social and cultural development.

The life unfailing needs to be channelled to each passing age; the truth unchanging needs to be expressed and re-expressed in ways that each age can appreciate. Christ is the contemporary of all: he speaks all languages, adopts all garbs. His Spirit, who clarifies the truth Christ taught us, who diffuses the life Christ won for us, is sensitive to every need of human kind. The Spirit says into the ear of the Church: "Don't ask anybody to cease being a man in order to be a Christian. Don't ask anyone to sacrifice everything he has ever loved, all the values he has ever prized, for the love of Christ. Rather, let Christ's love cast its life-giving rays on the soil of man's achievements to bring forth a harvest of glory unto God."

A year or so ago a newly ordained priest came to me and said: "Now I'm going on the parish, what works of theology do you recommend I read?" I replied: "None. For the first year at least, none. You have just completed four years theology. You must now learn all you can about *man* so that your theology becomes *relevant*. You are going out to build up the Christian community: you must know all the forces that cement and divide, that support and torment your people." I gave him a list of books on sociology, child-psychology, social psychology and the like. He returned a year later with grateful and generously glowing eyes—a rare occurrence! His theology had come alive: he had something to theologize about. God had stepped out of the musty pages of manuals on to the pavement of London's East End.

What are the forces at work in our world? What are the present achievements of mankind which are his attempt to solve the riddle and the enigma of his own existence?

We cannot pretend to give an exhaustive list. We can only select a few of these marvellous forces and achievements.

The exploration of the macrocosm

The modern world is larger than that of our ancestors. The earth is a sphere, 8,000 miles in diameter, one of nine planets orbiting a much more massive body, the sun, which form the solar system.

Between us and the sun around which we revolve at a relative speed of 70,000 m.p.h. is a distance of 93 million miles.

Man's great achievements to date are to film Mars at close quarters, and to send a rocket to the moon, the earth's satellite, a quarter the size of the earth.

Our sun is not unique. It is only one tiny star in the universe. It is a hundred times larger in diameter than the earth, but it is quite a midget compared with some other suns.

The most powerful telescopes we have show something like 200 million, million, million stars, all sources of energy radiating heat. The *nearest* is so far away that if we went from the earth at the speed of light, 186,000 miles a second, it would take us four years to get there.

The stars vary in size from bodies smaller than the earth to bodies larger than the whole solar system, and many of these distant stars are, no doubt, the centre of planetary systems as the sun is.

Within our galaxy, the Milky Way, the sun and the solar system are not still but moving perpetually, and the Milky Way itself is moving in relation to the other galaxies.

What is man in this immensity? More than four thousand of his kind would have to stand on one another's shoulders to reach the top of Everest. In size he is infinitesimal. In chemical components he is worth a few shillings. What is his real worth? He cannot think himself out of existence, cannot contemplate his own annihilation. What is his destiny?

The exploration of the microcosm

Ironically, the Greek word "atom" meant the "indivisible", the "unsplittable". A still useful, though now inadequate, way of visualizing the atom is on the model of a miniature solar system. At the centre is the nucleus and around it revolve small planetary bodies called electrons.

The atoms cannot be seen by the most powerful microscopes. They measure only one hundred-millionth of a centimetre across. The nucleus is immeasurably smaller still. As to the electrons, how many make up one gram? 1,000 million, million, million, million.

Atoms combine to make molecules. In any cubic centimetre of any gas—the size of a small lump of sugar—there are approximately 27 million, million, million molecules.

The electron orbits the central nucleus at 1,400 miles a second. This means that the electron goes through 7,000 million orbits in a millionth of a second. By now our own unscientific heads may themselves have become solar systems, mostly emptiness, with scattered thoughts spinning round like satellites.

Certain things, at least, are evident. Matter is not the dense, solidly compounded stuff we once thought it was. "It is, in fact," says Bertrand Russell, "much more like the Irishman's definition of a net, 'a number of holes tied together with pieces of string'."[1] Since the mass or weight of the nucleus is 1,850 times heavier than the electron, and the nucleus itself is so exceedingly tiny in proportion to the atom, the atom is mostly empty space. If we were to compare the solar system of the atom with the macrocosmic solar system we would see that the atomic solar system is, proportionately, infinitely emptier. Matter is

[1] *The A.B.C. of Atoms*, London, 1923, p. 7.

only continuous to our unaided gaze. It is as if the planets surrounding us were to increase their speed fantastically and run wildly out of their even orbits, those nearer the sun keeping from us the light of its rays and those farther than us from the sun blotting out the stars, so that the earth seemed covered with a dark, continuous, impenetrable, all-enfolding mantle.

We know that the atom is not only a source of wonder: it is also a source of power. Mass, as Einstein realized, can be converted into energy. A cube of sugar could supply enough energy to drive the *Queen Elizabeth* from Southampton harbour to the Statue of Liberty and back many times over. And there are direr possibilities still. . . .

For better or worse ours is a technically competent, nuclear-scientific age. Professor Oppenheimer said that "the pursuit of scientific knowledge as a whole-time occupation is so new a phenomenon that 93 per cent of all full-time scientists who ever lived are still alive today".[1]

The exploration of prehistory

Man's universe is not only larger, more scientific than it was. It is now known to be older than it was ever before thought to be by the Christian West. Perhaps the present system—not necessarily the world's creation—commenced from five to ten thousand million years ago. The age of the universe is, in a sense, unimportant.

How old is man? Civilization is only five or six thousand years old. But *man* himself? He is the result, doubtless, of 2,000 million years of biological evolution. *Homo sapiens*, the fully human stage, began perhaps 100,000 years ago. Reason entered into nature. Human beings came, capable of speech and the transmission of truths, able to think abstractly, possessed of a sense of history, wondering at birth and death and after-death; and placating the gods that there were.

Darwin who first substantiated the processes of evolution has

[1] G. M. Carstairs, *This Island Now*, London, 1963, p. 94.

had a lasting effect on the way we think of ourselves and our world. We are bound up essentially with all the material forces that move this world. Christians not less but more than others need to ponder this truth.

Interdependence

The whole world is moving towards unification as a point of fact. This has largely come about by reason of economic development and technological competence. New methods of communication have made the habitable world shrink in size like Alice on the threshold of Wonderland. When, for instance, someone speaks before the U.N. in New York and the speech is broadcast, a listener in London 3,000 miles away will hear it a split second or so before someone in the U.N. conference chamber who relies only on the sound waves travelling more slowly in the air.

Most problems are international ones. An explosion in Vietnam could ignite a world war. If Burma grows rice only for home consumption, India starves. Discrepancies in living standards, inequalities anywhere can lead to tragic conflict. This is why—apart from sheer humanity—the less-developed nations need assistance.

Perhaps the key word in world-relations today is "interdependence". In a primitive society, a man could count on his fingers and toes the people on whom he depended for his livelihood. He cut down trees for his bedding and killed animals with home-made tools; he caught fish for food; he made his own clothes out of skins and ferns. With the few members of his tribe he built walls, planted crops, dug a well.

Today, I have only to look at the books on my shelf to realize how different are the times we live in. A thousand books. The paper was once wood pulp. It needed processing and haulage; and for both, motor machinery was required; and for the motors countless parts; and each part has a history of human handling and carting. The modern world is composed of specialists doing smaller and smaller jobs, "knowing more and more about less and less"—with everybody becoming more and more dependent on others in the process.

The progress of humanization

Together with technical competence we have witnessed, firstly, the immense growth of educational opportunities. For me, education is the prime factor in humanization: it gives us a flaming torch to light up the fairy cavern of our souls and the world around us. The mind is the highest faculty we possess. An *individual* may dispense with education and reach the peak of holiness. But it is unlikely that society will provide conditions of justice and well-being for the masses without educating them.

It is of interest to note that the first public library in England was built only in 1848. Not until the Butler Act of 1944 was it finally accepted that every child should receive education according to his age, ability and aptitude. As one book puts it: "The only real safeguard against corruption in public life and the growth of bureaucracy is an informed and watchful public opinion."[1] Education alone makes this possible.

The other sign of humanization is the advent of public welfare. It has its roots in social concern. "Between 1945 and 1955, 45 countries adopted new constitutions or introduced important amendments to their old ones. A major purpose of such constitutions and amendments was to lay down, as fundamental principles, policies of social welfare, and sometimes to set up institutions and make specific rules for carrying out these policies."[2]

Health on the national and the international levels is today of public, social concern. Carstairs in his Reith Lectures for 1962 wrote:

[1] R. K. Gardiner and H. O. Judd, *The Development of Social Administration*, London, 1954, p. 13.
[2] *Ibid.*, p. 32.

"We look back now with pride to 1940 when we as a nation stood alone against apparently overwhelming odds; but in the perspective of history perhaps equal importance will be given to the years immediately after the war. This was the time when our people attained a new level of responsible concern for their fellow-citizens, a concern which found expression in the provisions of the Welfare State."[1]

In modern war men die, children are orphaned and property is lost in unprecedented ways; and we understand what before we did not understand—at least for a while. God brings good out of evil. Did it need the carnage of two world wars to build our nation and other nations into something approaching fraternal communities, to arouse pity on a wider scale than ever before and humanitarianism so deep that society will not easily lose the impetus created by it? Could it be that the two wars have at least had a catalytic effect upon other historical factors and so helped parcel men up together in a way that nothing else has done since the beginning of time? We have only to think of eighteenth and nineteenth century England described so vividly by Dickens when paupers were often unceremoniously deposited over the parish boundaries at night so as not to over-burden the local rate-payers—we have only to think of the destitution of so many peoples in Asia today—to realize how far we in Europe and the rest of the North Atlantic area have moved towards social unification. Moreover, in the process we have discovered to our surprise that welfare provisions are the necessary buttress to economic stability.

The progress of psychological medicine

Dr Stafford Clark wrote in *Psychiatry Today*:

> In contrast to the relatively smooth and sure development of medicine in the sphere of tangible, physical disorder, the story of the affliction of mind and personality is indeed appalling, charred

[1] *This Island Now*, op. cit., p. 92.

with countless burnings at the stake, chequered with violence, cruelty and remorseless persecution, and dark not only with the gloom of ignorance and superstition, but also with the despair of unlit solitary cells, stocks, bars, chains and brands, and all the sickening paraphernalia of torture.[1]

Mental illness was in earlier days mostly confused with sorcery. When those suffering from it were not killed—often they were, in hundreds and thousands, sometimes at the command of popes—they were detained in places which wove their part of the strand of cruelty which stretched in our day to Auschwitz and Dachau. Bedlam was no less horrible than Belsen.

Perhaps the most impressive realization of psychological medicine is this—and religion should have expressed it earlier and did not do so very clearly—the human spirit is not made well if it is sick, nor better if it is well, by force whether physical or moral, nor by bribes, intimidation, threats and fear. Spirit is, by nature, self-evolving: it is something which *lives*. We can no more cajole and beat someone's soul into good health or virtue than we can make a flower grow by hitting it. A person will improve when he has sufficient motives for being good and less reason for being bad—and unfortunately there are many who have few or no reasons for being good, born and bred as they are in lovelessness, like seeds planted in a cellar where no sun comes. He will improve when in himself he experiences the power and influence of a love that respects his personality and individuality, and does not seek to improve him by brutalizing him whether by pain or pleasure.

Spirit cannot flourish through physical or moral force: drill is not self-discipline, conformism is not goodness or holiness. Researches, then, into the condition of sick and abnormal people have led to a deeper examination of and insight into the motives which activate ordinary people and assist the development of their personality. But if I wanted to express in a word

[1] D. Stafford Clark, *Psychiatry Today*, Penguin Books, London, 2nd ed. 1963, pp. 9–10.

what psychiatry has done, it is—and I am aware of its incidental aberrations—to increase one's *pity* for men.

The distinction of the secular and the sacred

The last factor I want to isolate in our examination of the world in which the Church is enfolded, is the distinction of the secular and the sacred. In what is broadly termed the political sphere, we see the distinction of Church and state.

Western society as a whole does not more approve of one world-view than another. The atheist is no less respected as a citizen than is a Christian; he is not suspected *because of his atheism* of being less reliable than God-fearing men, as once he was. Today in many quite respectable quarters the fear of God itself is suspected of being rather less reliable than atheism.

It could be argued—and I would myself be prepared to argue —that the distinctness of Church and state was the first and most abiding benefit which Christianity brought to public life. For that distinction, the first of our martyrs gave their blood: Caesar was not God. So the apotheosis of earthly rulers and emperors was ended. Conscience became more intimately a personal possession than it had ever been. Complete tolerance became for the first time possible in the world. Lord Acton expressed the same sentiments in the last century: "All liberty consists *in radice* in the preservation of an inner sphere exempt from state power. That reverence for conscience is the germ of all civil freedom, and the way in which Christianity served it. That is, liberty has grown out of the distinction (separation is a bad word) of Church and state."[1]

That the distinction has not always been respected by ecclesiastics any more than by emperors, the Inquisition showed. That such a distinction was made at all even *in idea* is the glory of the Church. This idea entails that it is better to deny the faith than to force others to accept it, for to persecute is the

[1] G. E. Fasnacht, *Acton's Political Philosophy*, London, 1952, p. 23.

worst denial of faith there is. It is better to parade one's unbelief and in this way tempt people to think that Christianity is false than to persecute the unbelief of others and so prove to people that Christianity is wicked.

The secular society in which we live need not become the secularized society of which we all disapprove. But there is the immense problem of knowing how to communicate with secular man when the rites and language of religion no longer speak of his vital concerns and so no longer touch his heart. No one has expressed this problem better than the serene, profound Dietrich Bonhoeffer in his Nazi prison cell from which, in the high summer of his life, he passed to execution.

The Church and the world

We have now completed our brief survey of some of the forces at work in our world. What shall we say of such a world and of the Church's position in it? Will Pope Paul's wish be fulfilled, "that the two should meet together, get to know one another and learn to love one another"? (*Ecclesiam Suam* §3).

D. L. Munby, in a short but stimulating study, writes: "Let us not fill ourselves with such a narrow conception of what it is to be a Christian that people will say that Christians have not even appreciated the grandeur of man's achievement; if we have not appreciated the grandeur of man, how can we adore God whom we have not seen?"[1]

Pierre Teilhard de Chardin tells us that the incessant objection brought against Christianity is this: our religion makes us inhuman, withdraws us from the ordinary ways of humankind, isolates us instead of merging us with the rest of men, encourages us to lose interest in the common task.

The objection forces us to reflect: Are we really people who believe in the human effort as such? I mean, do we truly think

[1] D. L. Munby, *The Idea of a Secular Society*, London, 1963, p. 90.

that what happens in this world is important in and for itself or is it important only as a means of getting to heaven? Do some of us still harbour a sneaking suspicion that the more imperfect and miserable the human condition is the better it is as a means of reaching paradise? Does Christianity "nourish deserters and false friends"? "As though," says Teilhard to the unbeliever, "as though for us as for you, indeed far more than for you, it were not a matter of life and death that the earth should flourish to the uttermost of its natural powers.... Our faith imposes on us the right and the duty to throw ourselves into the things of the earth."[1]

Vatican II—though its intent is pastoral and though it wanted to avoid Teilhard's evolutionary and, some would say, easy optimism—nonetheless speaks with the same fervour of the modern achievements of mankind. The dogmatic *Constitution on the Church* speaks of men "who are already more closely united nowadays by the bonds of society, technology and culture" (§1). The Church prays that "the fulness of the whole world should pass over to join the people of God" (§17). "She encourages all the good that there is in the resources, wealth and customs of all nations; she takes it over and purifies it, strengthens and elevates it" (§13). She wants "to resume the whole of humanity, possessions and all, under the head, Christ, in the unity of his Spirit" (*ibid.*). "There is an obligation on the faithful to recognize the inner nature of the whole of creation, its value, its orientation to the praise of God ... they must make vigorous efforts to see that the resources of human labour, technology, civilization are deployed in accordance with the creator's plan and the light shed by his word" (§36).

There is here a serenity of attitude towards the world, not the world in St John's sense of all that is antagonistic to God but the world as matter and flesh and blood, the world of which we are a part and of which the Word partook at his incarnation, the world from which the Son of God still takes some elements for

---

[1] *Le Milieu Divin*, London, 1960, pp. 68-9.

his sacraments so that, acting in and through them, he may transform men's hearts.

Clouds on the horizon

To look forward with serenity, however, is not the same as blinding ourselves to the dangers. There has scarcely been an age of history not horizoned by dark clouds and not peopled by men praying desperately for the winds to be kind to them and to turn. But the present pile-up of clouds is unparalleled, and never have the winds been more capricious and boisterous.

Here is man who begins as a microcosmic speck in a woman's womb, who lives his ever-vulnerable life on a splinter of the universe, possessed of colossal power to build or to destroy. Hiroshima and Nagasaki, cities that burst asunder, point their boney fingers to novel and not unreal possibilities of annihilation.

The Russians, we are told—as though we could possibly understand what it means!—have fifty-megaton bombs. (A megaton is equivalent to a million tons of T.N.T.) A single fifty-megaton bomb is equal to forty-five times the total tonnage dropped by the Germans on the United Kingdom. It was estimated in 1962 that if war should break out, in the countries belonging to the Western alliance 225 million people would die.

Just as we were hypnotized in dealing with millions of atoms and light years, so are we by the prospect of the countless dead. The Church has this spiritual problem: to awaken men calmly yet forcefully to the dangers of their state, to help them become aware of something too difficult for their imagining to cope with, and to pacify the great powers who like two Samsons eye each other hatefully across dwindling continents and are ready, if need be, to pull down the pillars of the world and perish under them. The situation is not without its poignancy for, to use an example from Thomas Hobbes, the great powers are like two antagonists locked in a room each with a pistol, each wishing to throw the thing out of the window but each saying to himself that if I do he may break the bargain, and that even if we do it together he may hold on to his or have another pistol concealed somewhere on his person.[1]

So there is not anything quite free from the possibilities of distortion. The world is unified but not in love. The world is more humanized by education and social welfare, yet even this is fraught with danger when the earth's goods are so atrociously distributed as they are today. Psychiatry can lead to pity, to understanding, to the freedom of the individual; on the other hand, it can be manipulated by propagandists or advertising agents intent on destroying the public's sense of values, and at the extreme point, by indoctrinators not bound by any ethics of brainwashing. The growth of technology can bring the relief of poverty: it can also create the collective man whose work is soulless and whose reflexes are conditioned by the few industrialists who own the machines. The secular society can protect us from ecclesiastical absolutism which is no less voracious than that of the state and which is peculiar in that it sometimes persecutes its own children, depriving them thus of even the satisfaction of martyrdom: the secular society can also degenerate into the most indifferentist, the most illiberal and the most pagan of all human conditions. And God whose might and majesty would seem to be revealed in all the heights and depths of macrocosm and microcosm may appear to the multitude as to Laplace, a hypothesis for which it finds no use: a world once beautiful enough to demand a creator may be thought to be *too* intricate and *too* beautiful to be in need of one.

Conclusion

This is the world, ambivalent—as ever—in potential, which must be won for God. To the Church, the Spirit gives "youth and continual renewal" (*Constitution on the Church*, §4). She is

[1] Cf. Butterfield, *Christianity and History*, Fontana Books, London, 1958, p. 119.

older than the oldest traditions and newer than the latest inventions. She alone among the religions of the world can survive transplantations in every time and every clime. She is, to quote Pope John, the "mother and teacher of all nations" destined "to humanize and to Christianize this modern civilization of ours" (*Mater et Magistra*, §256) and "to hold the world in an embrace of love, that men, in every age, should find in her their own completeness in a higher order of living, and their ultimate salvation" (*ibid.*, §1).

Mother Church has the patience to match the restlessness of the children of earth. But like any mother she must learn to speak to them in a language they can understand as they wrestle with dreams too big for them, dreams more intricate but sometimes no less fragile than wrens' nests and spiders' webs. She must show them that faith illuminates the reason they cherish and does not put out its eyes. If she succeeds in this she will be able to show them that their infinity is, in them, the image of God whose personal and plenary expression is the Word made flesh for us.

So we end, where we began, with a proclamation of Christ, the Light of the World. It is the property of light to be constant and unwearying in the speed with which it comes to us, whether we go towards it or away from it. No less constantly does Christ come to us, saint and sinner alike, by his grace.

He is, to use a last image, the solitary mountain peak in a low-lying land. The clouds of God's graces burst upon his head and the Spirit's waters flow down his flanks to irrigate our wilderness: and the deepest, broadest, most strongly moving channels of all have the names of the sacraments.

BAPTISM IN SCRIPTURE

THE AIM OF THIS chapter, as the title suggests, is to let the New Testament throw a little light on Christian baptism. Heaven knows some light is needed. We have all come across lay people who have their children baptized in much the same way as they might have them vaccinated. "Better be on the safe side," or "It can't do them any harm." And to judge by the Sunday afternoon goings on in some parishes, there are priests who don't rate it as highly as vaccination. It is a ritual to be got through, and there's no point in being too fussy about details. After all, it's performed on an unconscious infant, and it works *ex opere operato*.

This mentality contrasts rather starkly with the liturgy of baptism itself. It is true that the present rite has obscured some of its original features by compression. But it has still kept the basic outline, which indicates that the actual baptism was once the climax of a long period of preparation, where the candidate spent the whole of Lent being repeatedly scrutinized and exorcized, so that he should finally be ready, on Easter night, to be plunged into the mystery of Christ's death and resurrection, and be fed with the body of his risen Lord.

The liturgy took it as seriously as that because the original proclamation of the Gospel did. It is significant that the first preaching of Christianity in the Acts and the first writing of it in the Gospels both begin with the baptism of Christ by John, both look forward to the even more fundamental baptism Christ

will give in the Holy Spirit, and both finish with an invitation
to come and be baptized:

> Go into all the world and preach the Gospel to the whole of
> creation. He who believes and is baptized will be saved.
>
> (Mark 16¹⁵).
>
> Repent and be baptized, every one of you, in the name of Jesus
> Christ, and you shall receive the gift of the Holy Spirit.
>
> (Acts 2³⁸).

It is within that framework—of Christ's baptism by John, of his
giving of the Spirit, and of our receiving it in our baptism—that
we should look for some light on the meaning and importance
of this sacrament.

John's baptism

When the New Testament opens its pages with a "Baptizer",
it is not announcing something completely strange or unheard
of. Baptisms were common enough among the Jews after the
exile—as indeed among peoples of other faiths too—as an
expression of purification and renewal. The extensive bathing
facilities revealed by the digs at Qumran indicate the extent to
which these purifying baptisms were practised. There was in
particular a once-for-all baptism which was practised on
proselytes to mark their entry into the Jewish community. The
plunging into water was seen as a definitive break with the pagan
past and the beginning of a new life as part of God's chosen
people. It did not replace circumcision as the rite of initiation,
but it was regarded as of equal necessity.

What is new about the Baptist's ministry is his proclamation
that *everyone* needed this once-for-all baptism, the Jews themselves included. For it was no longer sufficient to be part of the
chosen people: God could raise children to Abraham from the
very stones (Matt. 3⁹). God's plans were coming to their fulfilment, and it was necessary to make the definitive step which
indicated that you were ready for it. The kingdom of God was

at hand, and it was important to be prepared to welcome its
king, the Messiah (Matt. 3²). The judgment of God was
imminent, and it was important to be part of the wheat, and not
the chaff which he would burn with unquenchable fire
(Matt. 3¹²). John presents himself as the last of the prophets,
announcing the end times, the conclusion of the old dispensa-
tion, and preparing the messianic community which would
inaugurate the new:

> Prepare the way of the Lord (Matt. 3³).
> All flesh shall see the salvation of God (Luke 3⁶).

It is not without point that this took place in the desert, on
the banks of the Jordan. Ever since the time of Joshua, the
Jordan had remained in men's minds as the point of entry into
the land of promise. It is not surprising that the prophets saw
the Exodus that led up to it as a blueprint of God's plans, and
looked forward to that other Exodus which would mark men's
entry into the final kingdom of God. This is exactly what the
Qumran community had in mind, when they retired into this
desert to prepare the way of the Lord. And it is this that John
was inviting his converts to do: to repeat the Exodus experience
at a deeper level, to enter the Jordan again, so that they could
make the definitive pass-over from slavery and sin and death
into the presence of the living God. He did not claim to effect
this pass-over himself; he could only prepare men to be ready
for it. But he did claim that it was at hand, and that it would be
effected by a baptism even more radical than his own:

> I baptize you with water for repentance, for conversion, for a
> change of heart; but one is coming who will baptize you with the
> Holy Spirit (Matt. 3¹¹).

Christ's baptism in water

The Gospel account of John's ministry at the Jordan concludes, in all four evangelists, with a description of his baptizing

of Jesus. The scene—like the account of the temptation which follows it—tends to embarrass us. Christ was God, we say, and he no more needed a baptism of repentance than he could be really tempted. The two scenes are a piece of play-acting, we think, which Christ acts out in order to give us an example of humility and fortitude in resisting sin. John's baptism was for sinners, and you can't put Christ under that heading.

Yet the New Testament has no hesitation in doing so. It is true that St Matthew is as embarrassed as we are, and feels it necessary to add the explanation that this was done "to fulfil all justice" (Matt. 3^{15}). But St Paul has no qualms in saying quite boldly that Christ was "made sin" for us (2 Cor. 5^{21}); and the Fourth Gospel expresses the same thing when it calls Christ, at this point, the "Lamb of God who takes *on himself* the sin of the world" (John 1^{29}).

It is that title which is really the clue to the full meaning of this scene. Basically, Christ's baptism by John is his solemn anointing as the Messiah. Just as the Spirit of God had left Saul and come down on David when he was anointed by Samuel, to mark him out as the adopted "Son of God" ("The Lord said to me, you are my son, it is I who have begotten you this day", Ps. 2^7), so John the Baptist sees the Spirit descend on Jesus, and hears the voice from heaven proclaim him as the second David he was waiting for. In fact St Luke's account uses precisely that quotation from Ps. 2 to specify the scene. This is the enthronement of Jesus as the Messiah.

But what sort of Messiah? In Matthew and Mark, the words that come from heaven are a deliberate echo, not of Ps. 2, but of Isaiah 42^1, of the Servant of Yahweh, the ideal Israel who brings his brethren to God through his own suffering and death: "This is my Servant (or Son, the word is the same), my beloved, in whom my soul is pleased. I have put my Spirit on him." I repeat that this is the theme in the mind of the fourth evangelist too, who borrows from the same pages of Isaiah the description: "The Lamb who takes on himself the sins of the many." In other words, we *are* proclaiming the Messiah here, as the Baptist expected. But it is a Messiah who suffers, who fulfils his task of saving men only by way of his death. His glory is indeed announced, and he is enthroned as the Son of God. But that glory will be reached only by the humiliation of the cross. The scene is a doublet, if you like, of the transfiguration, where Christ's glory is proclaimed in the same words ("This is my beloved Son"), but it is framed within the three predictions of the passion.

In that light, the waters of this baptism should remind us not only of cleansing and renewal, but of all the overtones the word has in the psalms. In the psalter, water is a symbol of suffering and distress, the depths from which God alone can rescue a man:

> Save me O God, for the waters have come up to my neck.
> I sink in deep mire, where there is no foothold;
> I have come into deep waters, and the flood sweeps over me.
> > Ps. 69 (68)
> All your torrents and all your waves have swept over me.
> > Ps. 42 (41)
> De profundis clamavi ad te Domine. Ps. 130 (129)

It is in these waters that Christ has to be submerged; he uses the same figure of speech to say so himself:

> I have a baptism with which I must be baptized, and how I am in anguish until it is accomplished (Luke 12[50]).
> Are you able to be baptized with the baptism wherewith I must be baptized? (Mark 10[38])

It is only after he has been into the *depths* of this anguish and distress, and come forth from them, that he will fulfil the task he came to do. St Paul applies that quotation from Ps. 2, not to the baptism, but to the resurrection which it foretold:

> What God promised to our fathers he has fulfilled for us by raising up Jesus, as it is written in the second psalm, Thou art my son, *today* have I begotten thee (Acts 13[33]).
> He was made Son of God in power, according to the Holy Spirit, by his resurrection from the dead (Rom. 1[4]).

In short, Christ's Baptism is not a mere condescending recognition of John the Baptist's ministry, a gesture which we need not take too seriously. It is a preliminary sketch of his work of redemption, an anticipation of the death and resurrection through which one who has identified himself with sin will be transformed and filled with the Spirit, and declared to be in the full sense the Son who pours out the Spirit of God foretold by the Baptist. Or as Matthew puts it: "When Jesus was baptized, he *rose* from the water (ascended from the depths), the heavens were opened, the Spirit came down on him, and a voice from heaven said, This *is* (now) my beloved Son" (Matt. 3[16-17]).

Christ's baptism in blood

But why a death? Why did Christ have to die in order to be able to baptize us in the Spirit? Here we are touching the very central mystery of God's plan of salvation, and it is important to be clear. Why did man need saving anyway? What is the salvation or redemption that he stood in need of? How was it effected?

We have become used to thinking of the redemption in terms of a debt being paid, of a satisfaction being made to right the balance of justice. God had been offended, and justice demanded that reparation be made; and indeed an infinite reparation, because God is infinite. Christ was the only person able to make this, because he was God. So redemption was something done by Christ. By dying instead of us, by substituting himself for us on the cross, he paid the debt we owed.

Now this may be a legitimate way of considering the work of redemption. But compared with the scriptural explanation of it, it is rather thin. According to the New Testament, what was wrong with man was not that he had fallen into debt, but that he was utterly separated from God. What was wrong with man was not that God was demanding a price too great for him to pay, but that man had put himself into a completely different world. What was wrong with man was not that he stubbornly refused to be reconciled to God, but that he simply could not be. The New Testament supposes a situation which cannot be patched up by the legal fiction of imputing something to man from the outside. It is a situation which demands a radical change *in man* himself. And it says that this was effected not *by* Christ, but *in* Christ. Redemption is something which is accomplished by God the Father.

The words used by the New Testament to express this are "spirit" and "flesh". The terms are opposites; one is the direct contradiction of the other. "Spirit" is the word which describes the reality of God: his transcendent life and power and glory and holiness. "Flesh" is the antithesis of this, and comprises everything that lies outside of God. That does not in itself make it something evil; only weak, dependent, frail and perishable. But when this flesh rebels against God and tries to be independent of him, then it has cut itself off from the only source of life and holiness, and must tend towards death, drawn there by its own weight. In scripture, "man in the flesh" is the son of the Adam who sinned. Separated from God, and left only to his own resources, he can only rush to his own death and the final exclusion from the life which God is. Flesh and spirit remain incompatible. That which is born of the flesh is flesh (John 3[6]), and cannot possess the kingdom of God (1 Cor. 15[50]). The spirit is what is of heaven and the flesh what is of earth, and while the flesh remains flesh the two cannot meet.

Now Christ *became* flesh. We have to take this sentence of St John's seriously—I mean more seriously than we generally tend to. Our general tendency is to concentrate so exclusively on Christ's divinity that we become almost monophysite in our neglect of his human nature. We forget, or prefer not to remember, that his human nature was as truly human as ours. The New Testament—let me repeat—does not hesitate to say that he "came in the flesh" (1 John 4[2]), that he was "sent in the likeness of sinful flesh" (Rom. 8[3]), that he came "under a curse like us" (Gal. 3¹³), even that he "became sin" (2 Cor. 5²¹). In other words, he became one with us in this situation of weakness, godlessness and lack of glory. "Christ took his place," says Durwell, "outside the holiness of God . . . Christ could have said with his apostle: while we are in the body, we are in exile from the Lord (2 Cor. 5⁶)." He accepted all the consequencies of this situation, including death, which is inevitable culmination of existence according to the flesh. "The words 'flesh' and 'death' mean separation from God, deprivation of the lifegiving glory of God . . . He had to go back to his Father, and he had to take a hard road to get there, that of renouncing his earthly existence."[1]

That is what we mean by Christ's death. For us, death is merely the natural conclusion of life in the flesh; it is a death *because* of the flesh and sin. For Christ it was a death *to* the flesh and sin (Rom. 6¹⁰). Death set him free from the flesh, and allowed the glory which was his to shine through his manhood, allowed the Spirit he possessed to penetrate fully his humanity. His death was a pass-over, a transition from the sin-world to the God-world, from the flesh to the Spirit.

To put it another way, the redemption that man needed was not a mere improvement in status, a mere conversion from one state to a higher one. He needed a total transformation, by which he would be lifted out of this world of flesh and sin and death, and brought within the sphere of the Spirit, the sphere of God. And this was effected first of all in the humanity of Christ:

> It is only when I am lifted up on the cross that I will draw all men to myself (John 12³²).
> Out of my side shall flow rivers of living water. This he said of the Spirit which those who believed in him were to receive. The Spirit had not yet been given because Jesus was not yet glorified (John 7³⁸⁻³⁹).
> When Jesus had received the vinegar, he said, It is achieved, and bowing his head he *gave up* the Spirit (John 19³⁰).

[1] *The Resurrection*, London, 1960, pp. 47–8.

Christ's baptism in the Spirit

That is why the resurrection cannot be separated from the crucifixion. The title of this section, "Christ's baptism in the Spirit", is meant to be a description of his resurrection, but from what has been said it should be clear that it is not really a different section at all. In terms of the redemption, Good Friday and Easter are inseparable. One is meaningless without the other.

It is perhaps an indication of how thin our theology had become, until not so very long ago, that the resurrection played a very small part in it. And indeed, as long as the cross was seen in legal, penal, satisfactional, substitutional terms, there seemed little need for a resurrection. All that was required for a redemption had been done on Calvary. The debt was paid, justice was satisfied, the angry God was appeased. The resurrection was simply an appendix for which no room could be found, a sort of bonus stuck on to Christ's already finished work. It was a useful proof of his divinity, but it played no part in the work of redemption.

Yet the fact is that the New Testament makes the resurrection the very centre of its message. What the apostles preach as the good news of salvation is not a Christ who had paid a debt by undergoing death, but a Christ whom God had raised from the dead to become our saviour. The resurrection is the climax of every apostolic sermon in the Acts. St Paul even goes so far as to say that for Christ simply to have died would have been useless. He would merely have succumbed to the final humiliation of the flesh and sin: "If Christ had not been raised from the dead, you would still be in your sins"—however many crucifixions he underwent before (1 Cor. 15[17]). It is only because his death led to a resurrection that it became a pass-over, a transition from this world to God's world, from life in the flesh to life in the Spirit. In that act Christ achieved the salvation which he himself was in need of. What had been prefigured at his baptism by John here became a reality. His Exodus was complete, and he crossed the last frontier into the kingdom of God where he could die no more. His humanity had penetrated the divine world where he was filled with the Spirit and shared God's own name: the title "Lord" is not given to him until after the resurrection. St Paul says that by the resurrection Christ became according to the Spirit something which he had not been according to the flesh, the Son of God in power, whose name is "The Lord" (Rom. 1⁴). In that act he had been given a name which is above all names, that all tongues should confess that Jesus Christ is The Lord (Phil. 2¹¹).

And it is in that act, therefore, that he became the redeemer, the saviour. Because that Spirit which was his had to be shared with a mankind whose trouble was precisely that it lacked it. Until now, as we saw, he had not been able to give the Spirit because it was hemmed in by his body of flesh: "the Spirit was not yet given because he was not yet glorified" (John 7³⁹). But now that he had taken that body through death, what was flesh had become Spirit. His manhood had become a bridge whereby the Spirit that was his could reach his brethren, to transform them too from flesh to Spirit, and introduce them into the presence of God. Through Christ the breakthrough into the divine world had been made, as it were, from the side where it was needed, the side of mankind. The thing which had made him one with us, his humanity, had died to the flesh, and become a lifegiving Spirit (1 Cor. 15⁴⁵), pouring out life on the dead. It is the risen Christ who breathes on his disciples and says: "Receive the Holy Spirit" (John 20²²).

In raising Christ from the dead, God had made a new beginning, a new creation. Here was the head of a new human race, a second Adam. The promises that God had constantly made to his people had been fulfilled: the true Israel, Christ, had finally been brought into his presence. Christ stood now as the firstborn, the elder brother of a new Israel, no longer according to the flesh but according to the Spirit, into which all men would need to be incorporated if they wished to share God's blessings. On Easter Day, God's plans had entered their last stage.

Christian baptism

It is this that the apostles announce at the first Pentecost. They did not think, as we tend to, that this new presence of Christ in the Spirit was something to be apologized for, a sort of second best to supply for the absence of Christ. They knew that it was a more complete and more penetrating presence of Christ with them, and that in that presence God's plans had come to completion. They themselves had just been impregnated with this Spirit which introduced them into the world of God: this was the "baptism in the Spirit" which had been foretold by the Baptist and promised them by Christ. And they now invited all men to come and avail themselves of the same divine gift.

They issued the invitation in the same terms as they themselves had received the gift: "Brethren, men were asking, what shall we do? Repent, said Peter, and be baptized in the name of Jesus Christ, and you shall receive the gift of the Holy Spirit" (Acts 2³⁷⁻⁸).

The name of Jesus which they were asked to acknowledge was "The Lord". The prerequisite condition was that they should profess Jesus as Lord, that is, that they should acknowledge that in his death to the flesh and his resurrection in the Spirit this man had entered the world of God, and that this was God's final revelation of how man is to reach him. To accept Jesus as Lord was to acknowledge one's incapacity of reaching God by one's own efforts, to dispossess oneself and to commit oneself utterly to what God had revealed in Christ. This was the necessary prerequisite. But the act that clinched it, that exteriorized and ratified it, that aggregated a person to this decisive thing that God had done in Christ, that inserted a person into this saving mystery—was baptism.

It does not need to be pointed out how well adapted was the original ritual to express this fact. Baptism originally was not, as it is now, by aspersion or infusion, but by immersion. The neophyte was not simply sprinkled or wetted with water; he was plunged into it until it covered his head as though he were in a grave. What he was trying to do was to re-live Christ's own baptism in water, blood and Spirit. What he was trying to do was to reproduce in himself the process by which Christ had made his pass-over into the presence of the Father, to participate in the conversion of Christ's own being. The work of redemption had consisted, objectively, in a death and burial and resurrection. To make that his own, a person must put himself into those acts, so that what God had done in Christ he would do in him too. The New Testament describes the ritual as a baptism *into* Christ (Rom. 6³), a grafting *onto* the dead and risen Christ (Rom. 6⁵), a putting *on* of Christ (Gal. 3²⁷), an identification *with* Christ to the extent that one becomes one thing with his Spirit (1 Cor. 6¹⁷). In Christ, by the gift of his Spirit, the baptized person can call God his Father. In his identification with Christ, the baptized person has become the temple of his Spirit, and the new-born child of God.

In one sense, this is obviously something that is done once for all. You cannot repeat this radical change a second time, any more than you can die or be born more than once. But this does not mean that once it has happened it is finished and done with. Precisely because it is not, as people tend to think, something done *for* us by Christ, but something done *in* us by God to identify us with Christ, it has to be lived out daily through a whole lifetime. One cannot be identified with Christ without encountering the enemy who fought with Christ to the death. One cannot be a witness of Christ's death to the flesh without oneself becoming to some extent a martyr.

In other words, in baptism the redemption has indeed

become effective in us, because what God did in Christ he has done in us too, and we have passed from death to life. But this pass-over of ours is not complete and finished in one moment of time. Certainly it is true that the baptized Christian is no longer in the flesh: since he belongs to Christ, he has crucified his flesh with its passions and desires (Gal. 5²⁴). But it is also true that as long as he remains in a world which is not completely united to God, the flesh will continue to plague him, and there will be a constant and bitter struggle to remain free from it and "walk in the Spirit" which is now his. His baptism cannot be repeated, but it must be renewed day by day as he continues to reproduce Christ's "death to the flesh" in order to be filled with the "life of the Spirit". It must be renewed, made new again, particularly in the Eucharist, where his union with the dead and risen Christ is repeatedly actualized. There is some point in the Church's requirement, as the basic minimum for a Christian life, of a communion at Easter or thereabouts.

What I am trying to say is that baptism is, in the last analysis, eschatological, that is, like all the sacraments it points to the future, to the final completion of God's plans. The baptized person has been incorporated into the messianic community. With it, he has left the world behind him and is on the march to the heavenly Jerusalem; but that journey's end still lies at a distance. In a sense he has even been introduced into the life of heaven, for he cannot be *in* Christ without being where Christ is; but it will remain a pitched battle to keep that a living reality. For him the last times have come, as the prophets promised, with the outpouring of the Spirit on young and old alike; but that Spirit will not have taken complete possession of him until he has taken his own body through death, and been raised again by him who raised Jesus from the dead.

There are many aspects of baptism which have not been developed or given adequate emphasis here: the scriptural symbolism of water, with its power of dealing both destruction and life—a very rich theme indeed; the Old Testament images which prefigure baptism—because what God does can only be what he *has* done—creation, the flood, the Red Sea, the Jordan, etc.; the community aspect of baptism, the fact that it incorporates us not only into Christ but into a people. . . . These are all elements which are not simply interesting sidelines on baptism, but are just as fundamental as those which have been developed above. But everything cannot be said in one chapter. The community aspect of baptism will be given much greater emphasis in the chapter following. Perhaps what has been said can be best summed up by repeating again the key-texts:

> John the Baptist said, I baptize with water, but one is coming who will baptize with the Holy Spirit (Matt. 3^{11}).

> When Jesus was baptized, he rose from the water, the heavens opened, the Spirit came down on him, and a voice from heaven said, This is my beloved Son (Matt. 3$^{16-17}$).

> But the Spirit had not yet been given to others, because Jesus was not yet glorified (John 7^{39}).

> Jesus said, I have a baptism with which I must be baptized, and how I am in anguish until it is consummated (Luke 12^{50}).

> When Jesus had received the vinegar, he said, It is consummated, and bowing his head he *gave* the Spirit (John 19^{30}).

> By his resurrection from the dead he was made, according to the Holy Spirit, the Son of God in power, and his name is Lord
> (Rom. 1^{4}).
> What shall we do? Be baptized in that name of Jesus, and you shall receive the gift of the Holy Spirit (Acts 2$^{37-8}$).

III

BAPTISM IN THE WORLD TODAY

PAUL TILLICH relates the following story:

> In the Nuremberg war-crime trials a witness appeared who had
> lived for a time in a grave in a Jewish graveyard, in Wilna,
> Poland. It was the only place he—and many others—could live,
> when in hiding, after they had escaped the gas chamber. During
> this time he wrote poetry, and one of the poems was a description
> of a birth. In a grave near by a young woman gave birth to a boy.
> The eighty-year-old gravedigger, wrapped in a linen shroud,
> assisted. When the newborn child uttered his first cry, the old
> man prayed: "Great God, hast thou finally sent the Messiah to
> us? For who else than the Messiah himself can be born in a
> grave?"[1]

Christ *was* the Messiah and he *was* born in the grave. He is
"the first born from the dead" (Col. 1[18]). It was on his birthday
from the dead that God gave him a new name, a name above all
names, Jesus, Lord (Phil. 2[9, 11]).

Christ, you remember, had spoken of his death as a baptism.
His immersion in the waters of the Jordan prefigured this
death. It was Christ who cried out to God through the lips of
the psalmist:

> Save me from the waters of the deep
> lest the waves overwhelm me.
> Do not let the deep engulf me
> nor death close its mouth on me (Ps. 69 (68)[15-16]).

God heard him and prised open the jaws of death. Christ was
re-born, re-generate.

---

[1] *The Shaking of the Foundations*, London, 1949, pp. 166–7.

Does the word "regenerate" seem too strong to apply to the Holy One of God? Does it not indicate a kind of purging or purifying process to be gone through?

It is not too strong a word, for in a very real sense Christ did have to go through a purifying process. That is what our Lord meant by saying he had to be baptized.

What did he have to be purged of? Our sins. He became a man to take upon himself, in his perfect innocence, the sin of the world, to become sin in his humiliating death, to become a curse for our sake as he hung upon the tree.

How obedient he was, even unto death, submitting himself as the first Adam would not do to the sovereignty of God.

This is why God raised him out of murky waters, and broke the teeth of death. This is why God justified him, glorified him, exalted him, "constituted him the Son of God in power according to the Spirit of holiness by his resurrection from the dead" (Rom. 1⁴).

Indeed, the resurrection was for Christ not a mere continuance of the old life but a new life, a life beyond the touch of death. The life of God which, in his divine nature, was given him by the Father from all eternity now at last was fully his in his human nature. Now at last having passed over to his Father through the Red Sea of his own blood he is Lord and Christ, he is finally "made perfect" (Heb. 5⁹), "made perfect for ever" (*ibid.* 7²⁸). His baptism was a perfect baptism and the Christ is washed clean of our sins. But Christ did not only rise with his own glorified body, since his body, the Church, was also washed and rendered glorious in the baptism of her head. Christ was the grain of wheat: until dead he was alone, but dying he brought forth much fruit.

Baptism joins us to Christ

Christ's flesh was opened up for us like a curtain drawn aside, and it showed us a way into the sanctuary of God. "Let us draw near with a true heart in full assurance of faith, with our hearts sprinkled clean from an evil conscience and our bodies washed with pure water" (*ibid.* 10²²). By faith and repentance and baptism we pass over from the world to the Father and follow Christ into the sanctuary. "This sacred rite (of baptism)", says Vatican II, "conveys the image and the reality of association with Christ's death and resurrection" (*Constitution on the Church* §7). Christ's very pass-over process becomes ours. We die and rise again. As truly as our sins became his, his death and resurrection become ours.

As on the cross Christ became one with us in our sin, so in baptism we become one with Christ in his justification. How well is this washing named a christening. We put on Christ, so that God sees us as clothed with the glory of Christ, sees us *as Christ*, as one person with him. We have no righteousness of our own. We confess that we are sinners. We humble ourselves "under the mighty hand of God" (1 Pet. 5⁶), "who brought again from the dead our Lord Jesus, the great shepherd of the sheep" (Heb. 13²⁰), and made him "our wisdom, our righteousness and sanctification and redemption" (1 Cor. 1³⁰). We cannot approach, we dare not approach the Father except in Christ, the beloved Son who is always heard for his reverence. Whoever boasts of his own righteousness is excluded from the kingdom, he is not saved. "There is salvation in no one else, for there is no other name under heaven given among men by which we must be saved" (Acts 4¹²). *Through* him the one Mediator, *with* him the one Son beloved of God and our brother, and *in* him the true vine we are pleasing in the Father's sight.

Baptism joins us to the people of God

However, though each individual of us is saved we are not saved *as* individuals. As Vatican II puts it: "It has not been God's resolve to sanctify and save men individually, with no regard for their mutual connection, but to establish them as a people" (*Constitution on the Church*, §9). This is why my treatment of baptism is really a treatment of God's people into which we have been baptized. And this chapter assumes the form of a question: What does the Church think of herself and her role in the world? That will enable us to see what baptism is and does, and what it commits us to doing.

The Israelites were God's people in the Old Testament: they became so in the desert, they became God's assembly or *ekklesia*. The children of Israel belonged to God because they belonged to Israel. They had, and they still have today, this wonderful sense of racial solidarity and the not unfounded hope that God cares for them as a people.

The Church's sense of solidarity is not weaker, though it is much wider. For it is not now the blood of the race which is the determinant of our membership of the people of God but the blood of Christ. We come under its saving influence by faith and baptism. In baptism we as individuals imitate the Church or, rather, we share in what has been done once and for all in the Church. The *ekklesia* to which we belong is therefore universal or catholic. "For as many of you as were baptized into Christ have put on Christ. There is neither Jew nor Greek, there is neither male nor female; for you are all one in Christ Jesus" (Gal. 3$^{27-8}$).

If we read the Acts of the Apostles carefully we can feel very vividly there both the sense of solidarity and the sense of universality. The Church felt one because she was one with Christ. It is true that the universality of the Christian community and its separation from Judaism took some time to be impressed upon the apostles' minds. It needed the real destruction of Jerusalem by the Romans to make final the break between Judaism and Christianity on the surface level of history though, as we know, on the level of sacred, saving history there is a continuity between the people of God in the Old and the New Testament. We, too, have Abraham for our father.

It was the institutions and the government and the ritual that had to go, in a word, the Law. It had served its purpose. The Christian community was one with Jesus who "suffered outside the gate in order to sanctify the people through his own blood" (Heb. 13[12]), and who in doing so fulfilled everything that was written of him in Moses and all the prophets (Luke 24[27]). He was the priest, prophet and king to whom the Old Testament provided faint but true pointers.

Christ is priest, prophet and king

Christ is eternal priest and eternal victim. It was God's will "through him to reconcile to himself all things whether on earth or in heaven, making peace by the blood of his cross" (Col. 1[20]). Unlike the high priest under the old Law who every year made the offering of blood for himself and the people, "he entered once for all into the holy place, taking not the blood of goats and calves but his own blood, thus securing an eternal redemption" (Heb. 9[12]). "Without the shedding of blood there is no forgiveness of sins", and "the blood of Christ, who through the eternal Spirit offered himself without blemish to God" (*ibid.* 10[10])—"the blood of Christ cleanses our conscience from dead works to serve the living God" (*ibid.* 9[14]). What joy it is for us Christians not to have to offer up day after day imperfect sacrifices needing constantly to be renewed. We have only to offer the one perfect sacrifice daily and in every place, for Jesus "offered his own body *once for all*" (*ibid.* 10[10]).

Christ is also prophet, the spokesman as well as the final and personal utterance of God. He reveals God and, in the deepest sense of all, speaks for God in every word and every action of his life. After his sacrifice, no other sacrifice is needed, nor is there need for God to speak again. There is nothing more he has to tell us after the death and resurrection of Jesus which expresses perfectly God's love for us. No more need for prophets to be sent crying in the wilderness for men to straighten out crooked paths and to make the rough ways plain. "This is my beloved

Son," says the Father's voice from the cloud. "Listen to him."

Christ is of royal lineage by his first birth, holier than David and Josiah and Hezekiah, destined to receive from God the throne of his father, David, and to reign over the house of Jacob for ever. His was to be an endless kingdom (Luke 1$^{32-3}$). It was, however, at his second birth from the dead that Christ came fully into his kingdom. Then did he receive the title reserved of old for Yahweh himself, the title of Lord (Acts 2^{36}) to the glory of God the Father (Phil. 2^{11}). Yahweh's anointed one, his Christ, is also Lord (Acts 10^{36}), and he is both Lord and Christ by reason of resurrection. The messianic psalms sing of this birth, and this anointing and this lordship:

> The Lord said to me: "You are my Son
> It is I who have begotten you this day.
> Ask and I shall bequeath you the nations,
> put the ends of the earth in your possession.
> With a rod of iron you will break them,
> shatter them like a potter's jar" (Ps. 2$^{7-9}$).

God is king over all the earth (Ps. 47(46)^{3,8}). David sang in his canticle to him: "Thine, O Lord, is the greatness, and the power, and the glory, and the victory, and the majesty; for all that is in the heavens and in the earth is thine; thine is the kingdom, O Lord, and thou art exalted as head above all" (1 Chron. 10^{11}). We can compare this with what the captivity epistles have to say of Jesus, the Lord. Because of his humbling of himself and his obedience even to the death of a cross, "God has highly exalted him and bestowed on him the name which is above every name, that at the name of Jesus every knee should bow, in heaven and on earth and under the earth, and every tongue confess, that Jesus Christ is Lord, to the glory of God the Father" (Phil. 2$^{9-11}$). The epistle to the Ephesians also speaks of the great work which God "accomplished in Christ when he raised him from the dead and made him sit at his right hand in the heavenly places, far above all rule and authority and power and dominion, and above every name that is named not only in this age but also in that which is to come; and he has put all things under his feet and has made him the head over all things for the Church which is his body, the fulness of him who fills all in all" (Eph. 1^{20-3}). No doubt then but that Christ is king and Lord of heaven and earth.

So Jesus is priest and there is no other. Jesus is Lord and holds the world in the palms of his crucified hands. No more succession of priests, no more lines of prophets, no more regal dynasties. Only one priest, one prophet, one king, "Jesus Christ, the same yesterday and today and for ever" (Heb. 13^8). All is peace and fulness and accomplishment on the day when Jesus crucified rises from the dead.

The oneness of Christ and his Church

Now, God's new people, the Christian Church, the community of believers, is made one with Jesus. It is this realization which is most vividly present in the Council's *Constitution on the Church*. The Church is mystically identified with Jesus's body and all of us were baptized into this one body (1 Cor. 12^{13}). As there is a oneness of all mankind with Adam so there is a oneness of the whole Church with Christ. As there is a kind of church of the fallen flesh of Adam, so there is a Church of the sanctified flesh of Christ. Christ loves the Church with a husband's love as his own flesh, and nourishes it and cherishes it "because we are members of his body" (Eph. 5^{30}). Christ so loved his bride, the Church, that he gave himself up to death so as to baptize her and wash her body clean from every stain. How could the Church cleanse us unless she were herself clean from every stain? This is why by our individual baptism we become members of the already baptized body of Christ. We become true children and, as it were, replicas of our mother, the Church.

Whether we are thinking of the Church as mystically

identified with Christ's body, or as the mystical body which is completed by its head, Christ, this image of the Church as body, as an organism, enables us to realize that the Church is not simply made up out of its parts as a clock is made up of springs and wheels and cogs. The Church is created from above by God and is not something that is put together by men. The Church *begins* as an organic thing living by the life of the Spirit and is not the accomplishment of men who have come to some agreement about beliefs and ways of worshipping God and the best modes of government. This is why we are sanctified and become God's children in so far as we belong to Christ's body which is the Church, just as the Israelites belonged to God precisely because and in so far as they belonged to the people of God.

If we think of the Church as being distinct from Christ and so not identified with him, or if we think of the Church as being primarily the work and accomplishment of men, then we will be bound to think also of the Church as setting up a barrier—at least sometimes—between ourselves and God.

Of course, besides the divine, there is the human element in the Church to consider. This human element may exasperate us sometimes and encourage us to say what a friend once said to me: "Why don't we all leave the Church and become Christians?" In our more peaceful moments we know that such a thing is not only impossible but a contradiction. We might just as well say, "Why don't we all leave Christ and become Christians?" "This body (of Christ) is the setting in which the communication of Christ's life to believers takes place" (*Constitution on the Church*, §7).

If we remain faithful to scripture we will never be tempted to separate Christ and his Church, and we will be able to understand why we can talk indiscriminately about being baptized into Christ or being "baptized into one body", the Church (1 Cor. 12[13]). We will also be equipped to understand what the ecumenical movement is all about: it cannot be a matter of trying to reconstruct or reconstitute the Church, of putting together the pieces of a divided Church as if it were a toy that naughty children had pulled to pieces. However divided *Christendom* may be, the Church is, was and always will be the sacred, undivided body of Christ. It is from Christ that the whole body is joined and knit together (Eph. 4^{16}) as a single, living organism.

This does not mean, as we shall see, that the one, true, Catholic Church has any reason for complacency at seeing the divisions of Christendom or that she herself has been unaffected by them in her inmost life, and this over a period of many centuries. A body may be one and still not attain the full measure of its growth.

Let us see the consequences of the Church's oneness with Christ firstly on the historical and then on the theological level.

Where the Church is, there is Christ

If some Greeks had come to the apostles after Pentecost desirous of meeting Jesus (cf. John 12^{20ff}) and not knowing of the events of the pass-over, what would the apostles have replied? Would they have said that it was not possible to meet Jesus because, although he had been raised by his Father after being crucified, and was therefore alive, he had ascended into heaven? On the contrary, the apostles would have replied, "You are in the presence of the Lord Jesus. He promised he would be with *us* until the consummation of the world." They would have said with Peter, "Repent, and be baptized every one of you in the name of Jesus Christ for the forgiveness of your sins; and you shall receive the gift of the Holy Spirit" (Acts 2^{38}).

Christ therefore is not alive in some distant heaven, but he lives by his Spirit in the midst of the Christian apostolic community into which men are to be baptized, to which they are to be "added" (Acts 2^{41}). The disciples, centred on the apostles and led by Peter, formed the nucleus of this community which Christ had himself fashioned in the days of his flesh and upon which he had afterwards sent his Holy Spirit from the Father's side. It was on the apostolic witness that men based their faith, and into the apostolic company that they were "christened". For the apostles had walked in the company of Jesus and had witnessed his resurrection, that mighty, saving act of God. If only we confess it, we, too, are saved.

It is important to remember that Christ's ascension was only the removal of his visible presence. He has not gone away from us, for he has come in the coming of his Spirit. Pentecost was the perfect and perpetual interiorization of the presence of Christ at the heart of the Church. The Spirit is not Christ's substitute, any more than the Father sent the Son as a substitute for coming himself. He who sees Christ sees the Father: he who receives Christ receives the Father who sent him. Likewise with the Spirit. He who receives the Spirit receives Christ and, through Christ, the Father also. There are, in fact, not even *two* comings, that of Christ and that of the Spirit, for the coming of the Spirit is, as we said, simply the perfecting of the one coming of Christ.

All this means that there is no special, privileged moment of history for meeting Christ. He is alive still, yesterday, today and for ever. He lives on in his Church, so close that there is a mystical identification between him and her. And this is why he is closer to each of us now than he was to the apostles in the days before the Spirit inflamed them and established Christ's presence in their hearts.

Even those Greeks whom we imagined visiting the apostles soon after Pentecost were not luckier than we. What did the earliest disciples do after their baptism? "They devoted themselves to the apostles' teaching and fellowship, to the breaking of bread (the Eucharist) and the prayers" (Acts 2^{42}). Are we not doing the same? Are not bishops the successors of the apostles? They are themselves the apostles in the Church in our days. The bishops look to the bishop of Rome who is Peter's successor.

"In him (Peter) he (Christ) established the fundamental principle of unity of faith and communion, a principle which would be perpetually visible" (*Constitution on the Church*, §18). This is why "the Roman Pontiff is the perpetual, visible, fundamental principle of unity, both of the bishops and of the multitude of the faithful" (*ibid.*, §23).

If we want to know if we are in the fellowship of God's people, we have to ask firstly: "Are we in communion with our bishop?" It is to the bishops that Christ gave "the charge of proclaiming the Gospel all over the world" (*ibid.*, §23). It is to their charge that the sacraments were committed. The bishops "control the bestowal of baptism, which grants a share in the kingly priesthood of Christ" (*ibid.*, §26). They are the original ministers of confirmation, the sacrament which binds the baptized more tightly to the Church by giving them the special pentecostal grace of the Spirit to witness to Christ, to be Christ's prophets or spokesmen in the world, to spread and defend the faith they themselves received in baptism. (Since "by baptism and confirmation all are assigned to this apostolate (of the Church) by the Lord himself" (*ibid.*, §35) it is all the sadder that in England for so much of penal times there were no bishops to administer this sacrament of Christian witness.) It is in the name of the whole Church that the bishop either personally or through the authorization given to his priests receives back the repentant sinner into the full communion of the faithful. The Eucharist is primarily the bishop's concern and "every lawful celebration of the Eucharist is directed by the bishop" (*ibid.*). He also dispenses holy orders, in this way perpetuating the sacramental system and thereby ensuring the permanent presence of Christ in his Church.

The bishops' charge is also to rule the Church of God committed to them with ordinary (not delegated) power, a power given to them immediately by Christ himself. Moreover, the bishops with and under the pope, like the apostles with and under Peter, form a single college. This is why if we want to know whether we enjoy the full fellowship of the Church we must ask not only: "Are we in communion with our bishop?" but also this second question: "Is our bishop in communion with Peter?" The bishop, besides episcopal consecration to the high priesthood, must also be in communion with his fellow bishops and with the head of the episcopal college. It is this communion that enables the Church to present a visible expression of unity to the world. It is this that makes plain even on the surface of history that "the Church is the sacrament or instrumental sign of intimate union with God and of unity for the whole human race" (*ibid.*, §1).

It has also been established by the Council that "together with its head, the Roman Pontiff—and never without this head —it (the apostolic body) exists as the subject of supreme, plenary power over the universal Church" (*ibid.*, §22). The decrees of the Council are an expression of this power. In all their pastoral activities but especially in the Council the bishops, like their predecessors the apostles, act "in the name of the Lord Jesus"; and their aim is to serve and not to be served, to move, like Jesus, among the poor, the sick and the sinners. In every way, they are our fathers in God.

We have seen, then, that the enduring union between Christ and the Church means that at any moment of time to come into contact with the Church is to meet Christ, to belong to the Church is, in a very special way, to belong to Christ. We now proceed to see the consequences of the Church's oneness with Christ on what I have called, perhaps inappropriately, the theological level.

The Church is priestly, prophetic and kingly

Christ, we said, is the eternal high priest offering his sacrifice whereby he was perfected eternally. What does he sacrifice to his Father but his own *body* offered "once for all" (Heb. 10^{10}, 9^{28}, 10^{12})? The Church being mystically identified with Christ is priestly; being mystically identified with his body it is a sacrificial offering.

St Peter says that Christians are "to be a holy priesthood, to offer spiritual sacrifices acceptable to God through Jesus Christ" (1 Pet. 2^5). "You are a chosen race," he writes, "a royal priesthood, a holy nation, God's own people" (1 Pet. 2^9). Not for centuries has there been such a clear consciousness in the Church that the whole people of God is priestly. There *is* a priesthood of all believers. It is, indeed, because the Church in her totality is one with Christ the priest, and is therefore a priestly organism that some of her sons are set aside for, and ordained to the ministerial priesthood. "This priesthood of the ministry or the hierarchy" (*Constitution on the Church*, §10) is different in essence from the priesthood of believers and not merely different in degree. Nonetheless, the ministerial priest simply expresses in his service of the altar what the Church *as a whole* essentially is, Christ's body perpetually offered in sacrifice to the Father.

We must take very seriously St Peter's designation of the whole Christian people as "a royal priesthood", all sharing in their various ways "the single priesthood of Christ". In the Old Testament there are two texts which speak of the whole of Israel as possessing a priestly character. Soon after the Exodus from Egypt, Moses went up to God on Mount Sinai, and God gave him a message for the people of Israel: "If you will obey my voice and keep my covenant, you shall be my own possession among all peoples; for all the earth is mine, and you shall be to me a kingdom of priests and a holy nation" (Exod. 19^{5-6}). Likewise Isaiah 61^6 says of Israel: "You shall be called the priests of the Lord, men shall speak of you as the ministers of our God."

The first epistle of Peter and the Apocalypse (1^6, 5^9) echo these texts, for no other texts in the Old Testament express the priesthood of all believing Israelites. In Israel, there had been a priestly tribe and priestly succession. It was thought, in general, that priestliness was a closed and hereditary thing. This latter idea particularly has gone from the New Testament altogether. There *is* a ministerial priesthood, but this priesthood is identified with that of Christ, the one high priest; and in this priesthood the whole of the people have a share in their measure because of their baptism. By entering into God's people, by becoming one with the fellowship which is identified with Christ, they all automatically partake of Christ's priesthood. As after the passover of the Jews, God's people was called "a kingdom of priests and a holy nation", likewise after the pass-over of Christ there is the same designation. For Christ "has freed us from our sins by his blood and made us a kingdom, priests to his God and Father" (Apoc. 1$^{5-6}$).

This is the theological reason why the Church earnestly desires "that all the faithful should be led to that full, conscious and active participation in liturgical celebrations which is demanded by the very nature of liturgy. Such participation by the Christian people as a "chosen race, a royal priesthood, a holy nation, a redeemed people" (1 Pet. 2^9, cf. 2$^{4-5}$), is their right and duty *by reason of their baptism*" (*Constitution on the Liturgy*, §14). Baptism joins us to the kingdom of priests, and in the liturgy, especially in the breaking of bread, we exercise our priestly role. We offer the saving victim of the world to God the Father.

It would be wrong, all the same, to limit our priestly activity to what goes on "in church". To be baptized is to have undergone not an ephemeral but a permanent change. We are incorporated into Christ *via* his body, the Church. We are changed in our inmost being. We are priestly in our very essence.

It follows that all our activity is spiritual and priestly activity. We are always joined to Christ the priest. "Through him then let us continually offer up a sacrifice of praise to God, that is, the fruit of lips that acknowledge his name" (Heb. 13^{15}). Even St Paul (who was not an enthusiastic liturgist) sees the whole life of a Christian as a work of spiritual sacrifice. He says to the Romans,: "I appeal to you . . . to present your bodies as a living sacrifice, holy and acceptable to God, which is your spiritual worship" (Rom. 12[1]). He exhorts husbands to love their wives as Christ loved his Church when he sacrificed himself upon the cross (Eph. 5[25]). He thanks the Philippians for the gift they sent him and speaks of it as "a fragrant offering, a sacrifice acceptable and pleasing to God" (Phil. 4[18]). He tells them he may have to be poured as a libation upon "the sacrificial offering" of their faith (Phil. 2[17]). It is clear, too, that St Peter thinks in similar terms, for he tells us that we are "to be a holy priesthood, to offer spiritual sacrifices (note the use of the plural) acceptable to God through Jesus Christ" (1 Pet. 2[5]). The whole of our Christian life is priestly and sacrificial because we are joined to Christ and so it all becomes acceptable to God. It is the pass-over of Jesus which becomes ours at baptism, ours as a continuous possession; and this makes even eating and drinking, gift-giving, faith, purity, into priestly activities, sacred offerings made to God through, with and in Christ.

Having seen that the whole people of God, being one with Christ the priest, is priestly all the time, we must next consider the Church's union with Christ as prophet. "Christ is the great prophet who has issued the proclamation of his Father's kingdom by his life's witness and the power of his word" (*Constitution on the Church*, §35). The whole people of God "have a share in Christ's prophetic office" (*ibid.*, §12). The episcopal college is successor to the college of apostles and as such teaches in the name and power of Christ; "but it is not the only agency through which he (Christ) performs his prophetic task until the manifestation of glory. He uses the laity too, and therefore equips them with the discernment of faith and the grace of speech" (cf. Acts 2[17–18]; Apoc. 19[10]) (*Constitution on the Church*, §35).

I maintained earlier that there is a ministerial priesthood

because the whole Church is priestly. So I would claim that there exist organs of infallible witness to Christ or a *magisterium*, as it is called, because the Church in its totality is an infallible organism. Vatican II affirms: "The universal body made up of the faithful, whom the Holy One has anointed (cf. John 2²⁰⁻⁷), is incapable of failing in belief. This is a property which belongs to the people as a whole" (*ibid.*, §12). The whole Christian body is permeated and "informed" (or made alive) by the Spirit of truth. This is why the whole people possess the discernment of faith which "is the cause of the unfailing adherence of the people of God to the faith that was handed down, once for all, to the saints (cf. Jude 3)" (*ibid.*).

Though there exists a sacred *magisterium*, the hierarchy has no monopoly of the Spirit. After all, bishops—even the bishop of Rome—begin as baptized Christians. Subsequent to their elevation they have no special revelation of which the rest of the faithful are deprived, or of which they themselves were deprived before their elevation. It is their magisterial *judgment* which is now in God's special keeping. We must grant fully with Cardinal Newman "that the gift of discerning, defining, promulgating and enforcing any portion of that tradition resides solely in the *Ecclesia docens*".[1] But if the hierarchy's judgment —and we are speaking of the bishops not as individuals, for as such they are fallible, but as a body—if the hierarchy's judgment is safeguarded from error by God, what is it that they make judgment about? Evidently, the word of God, the message of God. But this word, this message is handed on: it is a *tradition*. In order to discover what the tradition is, the bishops must make inquiry, for, to quote Newman again, "the tradition of the apostles committed to the whole Church in its various constituents and functions *per modum unius* manifests itself variously at various times: sometimes by the mouth of the episcopacy, sometimes by the doctors, sometimes by the people, sometimes by liturgies, rites, ceremonies and customs".

Coulson (ed.), *On Consulting the Faithful in Matters of Doctrine*, London, 1961, p. 63.

The faithful have been consulted before now, prior even to magisterial definitions. Why was this? "Because the body of the faithful is one of the witnesses to the fact of the tradition of revealed doctrine, and because their *consensus* through Christendom is the voice of the infallible Church."[1] Looking back on the disaster of Arianism in the fourth century Newman felt impelled to say that "the body of the episcopate was unfaithful to its commission, while the body of the laity was faithful to its baptism". He went on: "I see, then, in the Arian history a palmary example of a state of the Church, during which, in order to know the tradition of the apostles, we must have recourse to the faithful."[2]

It is not a question of the faithful being able to define the apostolic tradition any more than it was over a question of the laity performing the functions of the ministerial priesthood. But as the whole Church is priestly, so the whole Church possesses and gives witness to the apostolic tradition which alone provides the basis for any definition.

It was, as we know, the exclusive identification of the Church's infallibility, on the part of some theologians, with the power of the pope to make infallible pronouncements which rightly annoyed Protestants in the past. If we are not careful a similarly justifiable annoyance will come over them if we now proceed to identify the Church's infallibility—or indefectibility of faith—with the definitive pronouncements of the college of bishops. Vatican II has deliberately guarded against such a one-sided presentation by stressing that "the universal body made up of the faithful . . . is incapable of failing in belief" (*Constitution on the Church*, §12). This is a most noteworthy statement considering that these are rightly days of enthusiasm for the episcopal office. We must not, for any cause, detract from the prophetic role of the whole people of God nor minimize the importance of the *consensus fidelium*. To neglect the former role is to turn the Church into an ecclesiastical coterie instead

[1]*Ibid.*   [2]*Ibid.*

of the leaven of society. To neglect the *consensus fidelium* is to court the danger of neglecting an authentic instrument of the apostolic tradition, and so of watering down the faith itself.

The whole people of God is priestly and prophetic. But Christ, the head of the Church, is also king and Lord of the earth. The Church must also as a whole share in his lordship, in his domination over all, whilst we remember, naturally, that it is a spiritual lordship which we are discussing. It is in a spiritual sense "that the saints will judge the world" (1 Cor. 6^2).

As the college of bishops has supreme, plenary powers over the universal Church, so the faithful of all degrees share in the mission of the whole Christian people. This mission is to extend God's kingdom in the world. The pastors of the Church cannot do this on their own. "They are aware that they were not instituted by Christ to take on themselves in isolation the whole of the Church's mission of salvation to the world" (*Constitution on the Church*, §30).

The place of the laity in the Church

The decree on the Church gives an interpretation of the laity's role in the Church which is quite different from that of Mgr Talbot who, writing to Cardinal Manning, said it is "to hunt, to shoot, to entertain"—the modern version of which is "to pay up and to shut up". This new interpretation is going to be of revolutionary importance in the years ahead.

From Vatican II we can cull two principles which will enable us to pinpoint the place of the laity in the Church. Firstly, their task is "to seek the kingdom of God in the transaction of worldly business and the godly arrangement they give it" (*ibid.*, §31). The second principle which is relevant here is that the whole Church is a brotherhood.

Let us tackle the first principle first. The laity live their priestly and prophetic baptismal life in the family and in society. It is there that they have to build up the kingdom, "to make their contribution to the sanctification of the world from the inside" (*ibid.*), to be the leaven in private and public life. "There is an obligation on the faithful to recognize the inner nature of the whole of creation, its value, its orientation to the praise of God. They must help each other to greater holiness of life even by means of their secular occupations. The result to be achieved is the drenching of the world in the Spirit of Christ, the surer attainment of its goal, through justice, charity and peace. The chief position in the wholesale fulfilment of this duty is held by the laity" (*ibid.*, §36). It is the laity's duty to baptize the secular world, and then to offer it as a spiritual sacrifice acceptable to God through Christ (1 Pet. 2⁵), "to be a witness before the world of the resurrection and life of the Lord Jesus, and a sign of the living God". For this the laity must pray and practise self-denial, for there is no apostolate without sacrifice. The holiness to which they are called is not a second-rate holiness. All of us in the Church have the vocation to be perfect as our heavenly Father is perfect. All of us must sell everything we have to gain the kingdom which is like a pearl of great price or a treasure hidden in a field. "All of Christ's faithful, no matter what their rank or station, have a vocation to the fulness of the Christian life and the perfection of charity" (*Constitution on the Church*, §40). It is this holiness that humanizes the earth.

The second principle enunciated by the Council is that the whole Church is a brotherhood. It could hardly be otherwise. We are all sons of God in the one Son, Jesus Christ. All the faithful, therefore, have Christ for their brother; hence even the bishops who teach, sanctify and govern the household of God are brothers of all, and should act in brotherly fashion towards all. This makes for equality "when it comes to the dignity and action common to all the faithful with regard to the building of Christ's body" (*ibid.*, §32).

The bishops' task is not to dampen the ardour and spirit of the faithful. On the contrary, they must try to give the Spirit a free rein in the hearts and minds of their flocks. They must allow public opinion in the Church. The laity for their part "have the right too of making known to the sacred pastors their needs and desires with the confident liberty which suits them as children of God and brothers in Christ. Their powers of knowledge, competence, position, give them the means, or rather, the duty at times of making known their opinion on matters which envisage the good of the Church" (*ibid.*, §37). Just as the *Constitution on the Liturgy* credits the faithful by reason of their baptism with the right and duty of making their voices heard in the liturgical assembly, so the *Constitution on the Church* credits them with the right and duty of making their voices heard in the Church at large.

The bishops are asked to reverence the freedom of their flock, the freedom which Christ came to bring and finally bestowed in giving his Spirit to his bride. "Sacred pastors must acknowledge and advance the dignity and responsibility of the laity in the Church. They must be willing to make use of their prudent advice, confidently to entrust them with functions in the service of the Church, to leave them freedom and scope for action, better still, to give them heart to approach the work of their own accord. With the love of a father they should give considerate attention in Christ to the undertakings, the wishes, the wants the laity put before them. Pastors will be on the watch to acknowledge the freedom which is everyone's due in the earthly city" (*ibid.*, §37).

Lord Acton once said of the Preamble to the French Declaration of Rights: "This single page of print outweighs libraries, and is stronger than all the armies of Napoleon." There is reason to enthuse in equally burning terms over the chapter on the laity in the *Constitution on the Church*. There was never a finer expression of the family feeling and co-operation which should exist between pastors and their flock, never a stronger yet more gentle repudiation of all forms of clericalism which would confine the laity to the side-lines of the Church's activity.

If the laity are loath to exercise their rights and duties as missionaries and apostles, lax about accepting their responsibilities to the Christian community at large—and to speak honestly, this is not so rare—the bishops are even in conscience bound to enhearten them for their tasks. They must encourage a sincere, courageous and prudent public opinion in the Church, otherwise, as Rahner puts it, "they run the risk of directing her from a soundproof ivory tower, instead of straining their ears to catch the voice of God which can also be audible within the clamour of our times".[1] Public opinion when it is not reverently heeded is always likely to decline into public, and sometimes——and this is far worse—private subversion.

Knowing where best to set the limits to public opinion is always a fine art. It must not be so narrow as to shackle the intelligent and hinder progress, convincing everyone that the Church is no place for men with minds of their own. It must not be so broad as to disturb the faithful to such a marked extent that the foundations of the Church seem to them to have collapsed—though, evidently, there are some convictions and practices prevalent at times among a good number of the faithful which do need virile though ever gentle handling.

What is most impressive and consoling about the Council's chapter on the laity is its insistence that the freedom accorded them is not a concession made to the democratic spirit of the times: it is their birthright as children of God. They have been set free not by peoples and governments instituting new social forms but by the Spirit of God. The bishop's duty of interrogating and consulting the laity, of co-operating with them in brotherly love, of sharpening by all available means their sense of responsibility for the whole Church, is made a matter of Christian principle. The bishop can never think that the lower clergy are simply there to work and the laity to pay: that would mean that he is being unfaithful to the apostolic ministry conferred by God upon him. Rather, he should look upon his

[1] *Free Speech in the Church*, London, 1959, pp. 14–15.

diocese as a rich and open field for the operation of the Spirit whose harvest it is his task as high priest to offer to God.

The bishops, we know, are the teachers of the Church of God. The education of the faithful in the faith *on all levels* is one of their primary concerns. It is not enough for the children to know their catechism; the highly intelligent must be encouraged to study theology. In fact, there are movements afoot amongst the educated laity to do just that. This must not be looked at as a subtle desire to undermine hierarchical authority. Nothing should be more pleasing to the episcopal body than this, for it is only when the study of the faith in the higher reaches is sound that the teaching given the little ones will be adequate. This is an elementary principle of educational theory. Educational competence percolates downwards. If the universities are deficient, it is unlikely that the schools will flourish.

The ideal is for the hierarchy to be supported by a well-informed and theologically serious Catholic public opinion. The teaching Church cannot be in a happy state, writes Newman, "when she cuts off the faithful from the study of her divine doctrines and the sympathy of her divine contemplations, and requires from them a *fides implicita* in her word, which in the educated classes will terminate in indifference, and in the poorer in superstition".[1]

Loyalty to the shepherds of the flock

To complete the picture of bishop-laity co-operation, we must emphasize the loyalty that the flock must show to their shepherd. Once the laity are satisfied that their rulers are informed of their needs and apprised of their suggestions they "should be prompt to welcome in a spirit of Christian obedience the decisions the sacred pastors make as masters and directors in the Church, for they are the representatives of Christ" (*Constitution on the Church*, §37). The authority of the bishops

[1] *On Consulting the Faithful*, op. cit., p. 25.

is not lessened by consultation, nor is the freedom of the faithful limited by obedience. This principle which is accepted in every well-run family applies all the more to the household of the faith which the bishop rules as "father in God".

Patriarch Maximos of the Melkite Church in an address of 14 March, 1965 has expressed the principle with precision:

> In matters in which there is a difference of opinions and discussion remains possible on the theoretical plane, everyone is free to propose his point of view concerning weighty decisions which the higher authority is about to make. But once this duty of fore-warning has been fulfilled, nothing is more agreeable to God and more useful to men than to conform oneself to the desires of superiors. If, indeed, the Catholic Church may glory in anything, it is certainly in its spirit of order and discipline which allowed it to attain in the world an unparalleled spiritual development.[1]

There can be no doubt that this order and discipline of the Church is something that many of our contemporaries find engaging and often admirable. They may remark at times on what they consider excesses of order, and yet even this is a source of wonder to them: the Catholic Church manages to impose "too much" discipline when other denominations seem able to impose none at all. It is not for us here to comment on the methods of imposing discipline current in other churches, methods less strict than our own and subject to criticisms of negligence which are not always fair.

The Church as catholic

The question we should like to elaborate here is: What sort of a face should the Church present to the world?

Of course, the only adequate answer is, the face of Christ. The Church must express, through her sacramental and institutional forms, the Christ who is the saviour. Since she is mystically one with him, all the human characteristics she

---

[1] *Chrysostom*, Quarterly Bulletin of The Society of St John Chrysostom, Summer–Autumn, 1965, p. 3.

assumes must be scrutinized repeatedly to see that there is nothing in them which keeps back the unbeliever from a genuine confrontation with Christ. If the Church really is the setting for the communication of the life of Christ, it is our task to see that this claim appears credible by eliminating everything within her which is unworthy of her Lord and Master.

What must shine forth above all else is the Church's *catholicity*. Christ came to save all men, and since outside the Church there is no salvation, the faithful must come to a vivid consciousness of the fact that the Church is not their private possession but that she belongs to the whole world. She has a mission to all men. The Council expressed it like this: "All men are called to this catholic unity of the people of God. . . . All in different ways belong to this unity or are orientated to it— the catholic faithful, other believers in Christ and the whole of mankind, for all, by God's grace, are called to salvation" (*Constitution on the Church*, §15). The first purpose of the decree on the Church was, indeed, to make "a clearer statement to the faithful and to the whole world, of the nature and universal mission of the Church" (*ibid.*, §1).

I have wanted to insist all along that to be baptized is to be made a member of that body which is mystically one with the world's saviour. Baptism is not merely a washing away of our sins. It plunges us into the all-atoning death of Christ, and so commits us to the world's salvation. In a word, we are not merely saved by Christ, we are joined to the saving Christ. We become the body of the Crucified, to use Pope Leo the Great's phrase. Our horizons must be as long and broad as those of the Christ who said "I, when I am lifted up from the earth, will draw *all* men to myself" (John 12[32]).

The Church is catholic not only in her mission but also in her power of assimilation. Nothing of value in national rites and culture will be destroyed by her, rather it will be brought to fulfilment. "It is the purpose of the Church's prayer and work that the fulness of the whole world should pass over to join the people of God" (*Constitution on the Church*, §17). In the *Decree on Ecumenism* the Council is particularly concerned to apply this principle to the Eastern children of the Catholic Church. "It declares that the whole of the heritage, spiritual and liturgical, disciplinary and theological, in its varying traditions, is relevant to the fully catholic and apostolic character of the Church" (*Decree on Ecumenism*, §17). The Church cannot fulfil her universal mission unless, in imitation of the Word made flesh, she integrates the culture, the language, the history of the people she is addressing and trying to win into her own presentation of the unchanging message of salvation.

The introduction of the vernacular into the Roman rite is one further instance of the Church becoming more diversified in unity and so more universal. The Church must become more Teutonic for the Teutons, more Anglo-Saxon for the Anglo-Saxons—it would be difficult at the moment to think of it becoming more Roman—and everywhere she must become more *catholic*. This is the touchstone of the validity of any contribution from the local church.

In Japan, I was told, the Church was in danger of coming to a standstill in its missionary efforts for want of a Japanese liturgy and a catholic rethinking and reappraisal of Shintoism.

In the second session of the Council, Bishop Yu Pin of Formosa explained why Christianity had not caught on in China. "We did not know how to harmonize Christianity and Chinese culture," he said. "We rejected too brusquely their worship of their ancestors which was the concrete expression of filial piety—and Confucius who was the concrete expression of wisdom and morality." He added: "It is necessary to evangelize, to baptize the traditional Chinese wisdom in order to create a new Church."

Bishop Skandar of Assiut in Egypt, while praising the missionaries who have helped the Uniate Church in Egypt, was sad that they had so often ignored its proper history, spirituality, discipline, liturgy. They have educated the Easterners as if they were not Easterners, he said.

The sensitivity of the *Decree on Ecumenism* is the response to laments such as these. The decree is the standing reminder that there is a kind of uniformity which destroys catholicity.

Think of a household where the mother behaves like a sergeant-major: the children's toys must be regimented like new recruits, their tiny, white pebble teeth cleaned as assiduously as parade-ground boots and gaiters. There is, we know, an excess of tidiness which destroys the homeliness of home. A good home is not one as neat and orderly as a dentist's waiting room; and a good mother, therefore, is one who is tolerant of a certain amount of grime and noise. The same is true of Mother Church. She is a woman with lots of children at different stages of development and with innumerable funny or exasperating ways. We can only wonder at the immense and marvellous tolerance she must summon up to deal with them; and the home is all the richer for it. Diversity is not necessarily a divisive thing.

Unfortunately the conformist mind is not only a precision piece of mechanism under a bureaucratic or curialist skull; there is something of it in all of us. If only we would become as forbearing as Mother Church. We need to, for the mission fields with their local languages and local customs are not only at the ends of the earth: they may be no farther away than the end of the street, perhaps no farther than the end of the pew. What was written of the Churches of the East may have applicability to the churches of London's East End: "Variety in practice and custom is no obstacle to the Church's unity" (*Decree on Ecumenism*, §16). The rattle of beads at Mass—for all *our* more enlightened ways!—is still not to be interpreted as a flagrant advertising of heresy.

Unless the Church manifests her catholicity both in mission and in powers of assimilation she can have no hold over the mind of modern man who sees the processes of world-unification at work everywhere on the natural level. If the Church appears to him like the relic of some pre-historic tribe, with all the paraphernalia of medicine men, tribal gods and mystic incantations, and every detail inward-looking and defensive against supposedly alien forces—if this is the picture presented by the Church to the world committed to her charge, she will be severely hampered in her attempts to baptize the nations.

Are we so sure that the world does not think of us in such terms? Are we so sure we have done nothing to encourage such thoughts? How much of these words of Newman are still applicable: "Instead of aiming at being a world-wide power, we are shrinking into ourselves, narrowing the lines of communion, trembling at freedom of thought, and using the language of despair and dismay at the prospect before us, instead of with the high spirit of the warrior, going out conquering and to conquer."[1] The deliberations and decrees of the Council would seem to suggest that were Newman alive today he would be more than satisfied with the preparations for war, the high quality of leadership, the quiet, confident optimism about the camp and the glint of the sun upon breastplate and sword.

The Council has been most timely and providential, for even our own youngsters today rebel against any attempt to turn the Church into a sect. They will repudiate *any* religion that separates them from mankind. And they are surely right. It is not wise to try to safeguard our children, who must go forth at the end of their school days into a secular and pluralistic society, by building around them a barricade of what is little other than sectarianism. The Church must be presented as an ever-open city, as a most sensitive and discriminating Mother who does not change with every passing fashion; and yet who is able to perceive the deep meaning of all fashion, so interpreting the world to itself.

This story is told by a visitor to Mahatma Gandhi's mud hut

[1] *On Consulting the Faithful*, op. cit., p. 46.

in 1942: he saw a black and white print of Christ upon the wall, the only decoration there was of any sort. Under the print were the words, "He is our peace". "You are not a Christian," the visitor said. Gandhi replied, "I am a Christian and a Hindu and a Moslem and a Jew." Such a breadth of sympathy, such catholicity of soul, should be one of the finest fruits of Christian faith and baptism which join us to the *Catholic* Church.

The Church as servant

Much emphasis has been laid of late on the Church as the servant of mankind. This aspect of service—and its accompaniment, poverty—must also characterize the Church if she is to reflect faithfully the features of a Christ who was stable-born and crucified like a slave. It was the recurring theme of Christ's public ministry that he had come to serve and not be served; to be like the Suffering Servant of Isaiah 53 in giving his life as a ransom for many (cf. Mark 10[45]). "I am among you," he said to his apostles, "as one who serves" (Luke 22[27]); and he took off his garments and washed their feet to symbolize his putting off the garment of his flesh in the following day's crucifixion, which was his own and the Church's baptism.

The lesson is evident, is it not? Our Lord was never clearer. The greatest in the Church must become the least, the leaders must be the servants of all. This must be so if they are to represent Christ, give a credible and creditable portrayal of the Lord and master before the world.

Of course, what this means in the concrete in the life of any individual it would be indelicate to intimate. Each of us must examine his own conscience. Pope Paul wrote in *Ecclesiam Suam*: "The zeal for poverty is vitally necessary if we are to realize the many failures and mistakes we have made in the past, and learn the principle on which we must now base our way of life and how best to proclaim the religion of Christ" (§54). What was so refreshing about the Council—the second session especially—was the way in which the bishops took up the challenge the Pope had made them and accepted the burden of apostolic poverty which goes with their office, even going to the extent of criticizing their own past carrying of it. For example, the Bishop of Verdun suggested that the Church does not attract the poor because it appears to be rich and often is so. May the bishops not be compared, he said, to the rich man in the Gospel clad in purple.

I myself want simply to re-echo what so many holy bishops have themselves said: it is a pity that the bishops' dress—leaving aside their ceremonial garments—should express worldly, juridical notions rather than their proper evangelical role. It is all the stranger to me in that bishops themselves are normally the most humble of men, conscious only of what Augustine referred to so often as the *sarcina episcopatus*, the burden of the episcopal office. It is not so much for their sakes that a more modest dress is preferable as for the sake of the Church. Christianity is a sacramental religion: external things are symbols of spiritual realities. The bishop is *the* representative of Christ in our midst. In his bearing, his dress, his life, we should be able to see mirrored the face of Jesus. A good though not infallible test of later developments in the Church is to ask ourselves: if the apostles were alive today, what would they make of this element or that? Their memories of Christ girding himself with a towel to wash their feet and lying naked upon the cross would have been too vivid for them to have made much of the chief pastors who succeeded them in this Church "founded by a poor man upon poor men" being clad in purple and fine linen.

The point being made here need not be elaborated. We can thank God that the bishops who are greatest in the Church of God have proclaimed that they should be the least, and for the sake of their faithful, should show themselves to be the least as Christ did. In this way they promise to epitomize, as they were meant to, the Church into which we have been baptized.

We may add as a theological note that while all Christians must strive to acquire the virtue of poverty, and while religious take a vow of poverty as one of the counsels of perfection, none of them is so duty-bound to be poor as is the bishop, just as none of them is so called to the degree of imitation of Christ as the bishop is by reason of his office. Vatican II, which will go down in history as the Council which proclaimed the true dignity of the episcopacy, is also the Council in which bishop after bishop has spoken of a love of poverty and service.

Hence we find in the *Constitution on the Church* the following remarks: "Christ completed the work of redemption in poverty and under persecution. In the same way, the Church is called to tread the same path . . . for our sake 'he (Christ) impoverished himself, when he was so rich' (2 Cor. 8⁹). Just so the Church, while she may need human wealth to carry out her mission, is not erected to seek earthly glory, but to spread humility and self-denial, by the example she too must give" (§ 8).

We know—and the history of Europe provides abundant testimony of it—that the Church has often failed in this and in other respects. She has been unfaithful to her role of evangelical poverty and has sought after earthly glory.

The Church as holy and unholy

It might be objected that we cannot speak of the Church in the way we have done. Shouldn't we say that it is not *the Church* who has failed but *her children*? I think not. It is theologically incorrect to suggest that the word "Church" can be the subject of laudatory but not of non-laudatory qualification. This is not merely a linguistic question for it affects the whole way we *think* about the Church.

The Church has two aspects, the divine and the human. She is created from above, yet journeys here below. The Council once again has expressed the matter with wonderful clarity and exactness: "For all her richness of earthly and heavenly wealth, we must not think of the Church as two substances, but a single, complex reality, the compound of a human and a divine element. By a significant analogy she is likened to the mystery of the Word incarnate: the nature taken by the divine Word serves as the instrument of salvation, in a union with him which is indissoluble; in the same way, the social framework of the Church serves the Spirit of Christ, her life-giver, for his bodily growth (Eph. 4¹⁶)" (*Constitution on the Church*, §8).

Christ—although he possesses both a human and a divine nature and so both raises the dead through the power of God and dies upon the cross through the weakness of man—is the one Son of God. Likewise the Church—though compounded of the human and the divine, the sinful and the holy—is but the one bride of Christ. There are not two Churches, one sinful and one spotless. The same one Church is holy in so far as she is God's work, and sinful in so far as men have not wanted to co-operate with the graces channelled to them.

Pope Paul talked of the defects of the Church in this way: "The actual image of the Church will never attain to such a degree of perfection, beauty, holiness and splendour that it can be said to correspond perfectly with the original conception in the mind of him who fashioned it" (*Ecclesiam Suam*, §10). It is the refusal to qualify the term "Church" by any pejorative predicates which has led in the past to a certain Catholic form of pharisaism. "The Church is not like the rest of institutions" —even when unprejudiced historians tell us that she is. Of course, in very important ways she *is* different from other institutions, but the attitude we have outlined has insensibly caused us to make claims for the Church under aspects both human and divine which only pertain to the divine aspect. Triumphalism—however much the glory may appear to have been accorded to God alone—has been the result.

In the field of ecumenism it has led us to deny that the Church is in constant need of renewal: "This is the Church of

Christ, the immaculate bride of Christ. How can the *Church* be renewed?" Such has been our attitude at times and there is no point in denying it. Likewise, with dogmatic definitions: "What the Church has declared is not only irreversible, as all truth is, it is also unrevisable in any way." The consequence has been an almost irreverent attitude to God himself, since no human categories—however much vouched for by the Church —can even begin to exhaust the plenitude which God is, or to plumb the depths of the riches of the wisdom of knowledge revealed in Christ. Our statements about God can always be improved on and complemented by others.

Unless we are explicitly aware that "Church" can be a term to which non-laudatory predicates, even the term "sinful", can be applied, we may also tend to be lax in the scrutiny we give our own actions should we be in an ever so minor position of authority and acting "in Christ's name" or "in the name of the Church". These last phrases may make us blind to the most obvious defects in our actions and operations. We may even cease altogether to examine what we do with impartiality, or to judge it by any of the normal criteria of success and failure, or even of good and bad. The process of mind involved seems to be something like this: the Church cannot ever fail; I am acting in the name of the Church, how can I fail? Or: the Church speaks with Christ's authority; I am in the place of Christ, therefore I speak with Christ's authority. All the time, it may well be that we are perpetrating an injustice which a veritable pagan would discern as such, and are guilty of an insensitivity with which Jesus Christ would be the last to want his holy name to be associated. Even religious superiors are capable of taking the Lord's name in vain.

An example was given me recently of how easy it is—and without any malice—for the Church's legitimate authority to be utilized by those of lesser rank. A convent superior replied to a modest request for a certain change in the daily Mass routine with the words, "I'm afraid, Father, that Rome has recently decreed otherwise." The impression given was that the Sacred Congregation of Religious had made a solemn declaration on the matter. In fact, all that had happened was that Mother General had sent around her regular little circular to superiors about what was to be the daily programming of Mass and Office. Since Mother General had her H.Q. at Rome, "Rome" had spoken. Her authority would no doubt have sounded far less impressive had she established the Generalate in Bognor or Bootle.

Even when it is correct to say in one instance or another that Rome has spoken and that what is spoken is of highest authority, we must still beware of romanticizing or infallibilizing the decree. "And who is Propaganda?" asked Newman in one of his angrier moods. "Virtually one sharp man of business who works day and night, and despatches his work quick off, to the East and to the West."[1] Maybe it would be worthwhile to subject all the sentences in which the words "Rome speaks" or "the Church says" to what English philosophers call linguistic analysis. The results, I suspect, would be most revealing.

The purpose of this diversion was not to encourage disrespect for the Church and ecclesiastical authority but to show how a refusal ever to qualify "the Church" by allegedly unworthy predicates leads to a misunderstanding of her nature. Language only perpetuates the misunderstanding.

It is refreshing to see that the Council has put an end to this brand of Catholic pharisaism in the following words: "The Church, however, with sinners clasped to her bosom, is at once holy and in constant need of cleansing, thus she pursues a ceaseless course of penance and renewal" (*Constitution on the Church*, §8). Her holiness is at once genuine but imperfect (*ibid.*, §48). The laity are asked "to contribute to the growth of the Church and its continual sanctification" (*ibid.*, §33). And in the Decree on Ecumenism: "The Church on its pilgrimage is called by Christ to the continual reformation of which it

[1] *On Consulting the Faithful*, op. cit., p. 45.

perpetually stands in need, as a human, earthly institution" (§6). Catholics engaged in ecumenical activity "must first of all give their wholehearted attention to careful consideration of reforms to be made and action to be taken within the Catholic household" (*ibid.*, §4).

The council has affirmed—and it is something we were reluctant to say before—that the pilgrim Church is in need of "constant cleansing". The age of prophecy is over. The death and resurrection of Christ is the only standard we need by which to judge the events of history and our own lives; or, better, that pass-over event is itself the judgment. But had any prophets been required after Christ, and had they come to judge the Church, they would without a doubt have spoken to her at times as roundly as Jeremiah did to the Israelites who were the people of God and joined to him by covenant as we are:

> Also on your skirts is found
> the lifeblood of guiltless poor;
> You did not find them breaking in.
> Yet in spite of all these things
> You say, "I am innocent;
> Surely his anger has turned from me?"
> Behold, I will bring you to judgment
> for saying, "I have not sinned" (Jer. 2[34-35]).

The Church and Ecumenism

In these days, the Church who stands perpetually in need of cleansing and renewal is confessing humbly her sins against unity. If she had been more aware of the need for renewal at an earlier period perhaps no Luther would have arisen to tear the Church apart. The fathers of the Council speaking for the whole of the Catholic Church have said: "St John's statement has a bearing on faults against unity: 'If we deny that we have sinned, it means that we are treating him as a liar; it means that his word does not dwell in our hearts' (1 John 1[10]). Therefore we make a humble plea for the pardon of God and of our separated brethren, as we forgive them that trespass against us" (*Decree on Ecumenism*, §7).

The whole tone of this avowal is different from anything we would have dreamed of even ten years ago. The reversal has been so pronounced that one bishop felt called upon to make what is likely to stand as the most amusing remark of the Council, "These days, you can't even call the devil 'Satan'. He's 'our separated brother'."

Whilst avoiding such an extreme as this the Council does speak of a kind of recent awakening of the Church to the ecumenical situation. "The Church *has come to recognize* several reasons for her connection with those who are baptized and have the honour of the name of Christian, yet do not profess the faith in its entirety, or maintain union in fellowship under Peter's successor" (*Constitution on the Church*, §15).

That the whole concept is new to many Catholics is shown in the following story. A professor of dogmatic theology in an English seminary was holding a junior clergy examination not long after the publication of the *Decree on Ecumenism*. He asked one of the priest-examinees whether he had read the pronouncement. On receiving the answer "No", the professor summarized the main points of it and asked the young priest what comments he would like to make on what he had heard. Not realizing he had just been given a précis of the Council's words, the hapless young priest simply said: "I've only one comment. Such views are distinctly dangerous, Father."

"Distinctly dangerous" they would have seemed to any of us in earlier days, childhood days when either we or our parents were called "Roman candles" and taunted with the little refrain: "Catholic, Catholic, quack, quack, quack. Go to the devil and never come back." Whereupon we replied by bloodying their Protestant noses, thereby proving incontrovertibly that we belonged to the one, true Church of Christ. How cold the love of Christians for one another became is evidenced by the genuine amazement people show today at them now being nice to each other.

In any estimate of the Church's role in the modern world the duty of fostering inter-Church relations must rank very high. This, after all, was declared as one of the principal aims of the Council from the beginning. It is an aim which any baptized Christian must keep in the forefront of his mind: he must be ecumenical if he is to be a Christian, in that what is at stake is the very unity of the Catholic Church.

This has not always been appreciated and has led in the past to a kind of insouciance on the part of Catholics and their pastors towards the problem of reunion. The Church is one of its nature. She is the undivided body of Christ, The very "fullness" (Eph. 1²³ of Christ and knit together by the Spirit of God. The unity of the Church was meant to be an earthly replica of the unity of the persons in the Trinity.

This unity is not that of a dead thing but of a living organism. It is a unity that can be injured at times and improved on at others. Although it cannot be lost, or else the Church would cease to be the Church, it depends on us whether it grows or diminishes. The Council has said: "This unity was bestowed by Christ on his Church at the beginning, we believe that it is still in existence in the Catholic Church and cannot be lost; we hope it will *continue to increase* daily until the consummation of the world" (*Decree on Ecumenism*, §4).

The present divisions among Christians are manifestly against the will of Christ who prayed on the night before his death which was to bring all men into one (John 11⁵²) "that they may be one, Father, as thou in me and I in thee, that they may be one in us, so that the world may believe" (John 17²¹).

These divisions militate against "the full completion of unity, which is the desire of Jesus Christ" (*Decree on Ecumenism*, §4), and the object of his all-at-one-ing death. They "constitute a hindrance which prevents *the Church's own catholicity* from being realized in its fullness" (*ibid.*). They prevent Christians giving a unified witness to Christ and are thus a source of scandal to unbelievers.

The days of complacency are gone. The days when each side said, "*Our* consciences at least are clear" are gone. Our Mother the Church has admitted not only her own faults as one of the causes of division, but more important, she has admitted how much she is suffering in her very being because of those same divisions. Her unity is impaired, her catholicity is lessened.

This last admission is crucial. Without it, the Catholic Church could not enter the ecumenical dialogue with fitting enough humility. We are not merely confessing the sins of our forefathers of which we may or may not feel guilty. We are confessing our own sins which perpetuate a condition which affects the Church we love in her inmost life. We stand to benefit from ecumenism. The other churches and ecclesial communities have been used by the Spirit to bring forth a harvest to God. The true Christian values they preserved and developed "derive from the common heritage" (*Decree on Ecumenism*, §4) and these can be a source of edification to us. These are the things which, if we are allowed to share them, will enhance the catholicity of the Church.

This humble admission by the Church of the wounds caused her by separation is another reason for the beautiful sensitivity of the *Decree on Ecumenism*. Disagreements, it is admitted, are real enough. Prudence and patience are essential. We must beware of a false attitude of appeasement and are therefore in duty bound to state with the utmost lucidity and *completeness* what our own beliefs are.

Despite these necessary reminders, the Council speaks of our divisions as being between members of the same family, the same household. Are we not "brothers", though separated? And, besides, how deep are the separations? Deep enough, true, to wound the heart of Christ, and this is why we must pray and do penance for the cause of unity. Our brother Christians are outside the Church's "framework" (*Constitution on the Church*, §8), and this is painful to us. Nevertheless, there is much cause for comfort and brotherly feeling between us. "Men who believe in Christ and who have duly received baptism are established in a fellowship with the Catholic Church, even if the fellowship be incomplete" (*Decree on Ecumenism*, §3). This fellowship has different degrees.

Firstly, the Council speaks with the utmost respect of the Churches of the East with whom our fellowship is deepest. Orthodoxy, with its apostolic succession, possesses the priesthood and the Eucharist. This possession of theirs keeps them connected to us by the closest degree of kinship. Given appropriate circumstances, therefore, and the approval of ecclesiastical authority, some sharing in sacred rites is not only possible but advisable" (*ibid.*, §15). This extends even to a communal Eucharist.

But even with our brother Christians in the West we have many things in common. To begin with, baptism "sets up a sacramental bond of unity existing among all those who have had rebirth through him (Christ)" (*ibid.*, §22). If baptism is genuine, it must cause a true faith. How could there be Christian baptism without faith in the Trinity and in the one Mediator between God and men, Jesus Christ? That the faith of our fellow-Christians is true is proved on another score: without Christian faith there can be no true Christian hope or love, which are built up on the foundation of faith. And who would dare to dispute the validity of our brother Christians' hope and charity? "But," continues the *Decree*, "in itself, baptism is only a beginning, an introduction, for it is wholly directed to the acquisition of the fulness of life in Christ. Baptism is oriented to the complete profession of faith, the complete incorporation in the institute of salvation as Christ wanted, the complete integration into the fellowship of the Eucharist" (§22).

We Catholics are not only called to foster relationships with our fellow Christians but to "*take the first step towards them*" (*ibid.*, §4). We must not hold aloof, hoping that if we remain intransigent, eventually in God's good time they will see the light. The Catholic Church is wanting to open wide her arms and to go to meet the sons who belong to her and have been too long away from her bosom. The bishops are called upon to promote ecumenism energetically, "and to give it their prudent, personal direction" (*ibid.*, §4). It is for the bishops as successors of the apostles to arrange for the discussions of theological questions "on a basis of equality" (*ibid.*, §9), and for joint public prayer which "is not only lawful but desirable". Such prayers in common "are an authentic expression of the ties which still attach Catholics to their separated brethren" (*ibid.*, §8), and will certainly move God whose Holy Spirit has called the movement into being to answer fully Christ's prayer for unity on the night before he died.

Christ's prayer for unity, by the process of identification, becomes the Church's prayer; and in this prayer every baptized Christian joins. The Church is priestly and prophetic and kingly and missionary; and each one of us is a Catholic in so far as he participates in every role of his Mother. The unity of the Church exists so that the world may believe (John 17[21]). Unity is the indispensable condition of bringing Christ to the world. If we Christians cannot heal our own divisions, can we heal the world's? It is pertinent to ask, Have we, while still divided, any message for the divided world at all? All we can say is that at least more progress has been made at Rome lately than at Geneva. But a long road stretches ahead, leading across swampland and high up over mountains.

The genuine concern of Christians for each other, their determination to co-operate in moral and social action and to engage in the sciences and the arts in a Christian spirit, provides at least a temporary basis for a dignified and unified approach to the world.

The Church and human values

As to the Church herself, there is need of a much greater emphasis on purely human values both intellectual and practical. Churchmen must show that they really do hold to the freedom of the individual, integrity of mind, disinterestedness of research, trust in the intelligence. It is so easy to give but a grudging or notional assent to such things, the proof of this being that when the Church's causes or interests seem to be in the slightest way endangered nobody seems to be very interested in them any more, or perhaps positive steps are taken to suppress them. Theoretically the Church has always stood for the harmony of faith and reason, but it would be foolish to deny the innumerable instances when reason has had to take an uncalled-for buffeting.

In practical affairs, the Church must lead the way in the corporal works of mercy. On this score, we shall have more to say in our chapter on "The Eucharist in the World Today".

The Church's problem—like any other institution's—is to mobilize all her hidden forces. Perhaps no other society in history has ever produced so much dedication with so little enthusiasm—an incredible combination. Often the enthusiasm has been lacking because there was no outlet for it. The Catholic Church with its million nuns and its numberless lay-folk on whom the Spirit has descended is like a huge plot of land hitherto faithfully farmed but yielding relatively little in the way of produce. And now rich seams of uranium have been discovered in its depths, giving unsuspected sources of power.

The machinery needed to mine this uranium-power is education. *The basic problem of the Catholic Church in our day above all days is that of education.* Whilst our priests are educated outside the mainstream of the nation's cultural life, whilst many intelligent young women in convents receive a cultural formation which will only fit them for the kitchen, we shall, to adopt political jargon, never be anything more than a second-rate power in the world. Movements are afoot to remedy our past deficiencies, but it is an understatement to say that perhaps Achilles was a little fleeter.

The Church has insisted of late that she is no provincial troupe of players performing regularly and unconvincingly before the local shopkeepers and the local spinsters. Her task is to play before the whole world. She has a mission to all. This is why "she encourages all the good that there is in the resources, wealth and customs of the nations; she takes it over and purifies it, strengthens and elevates it" (*Constitution on the Church*, §13). Without education, without a profound knowledge of the faith and of human science and culture, no marriage between the Church and the world is possible. The two will always seem opposed and be suspicious of each other. But the marriage, if it comes about at all, will be arranged by the laity in whom Church and world are already so closely allied. The Council repeated this idea often. "On all the laity, then, falls the glorious burden of toiling to bring the divine offer of salvation ever more and more into the reach of all men of all times and all over the world" (*ibid.*, §33). Theirs is to "steep human culture and activity in moral value" (*ibid.*, §36). Theirs is to baptize the earth with all its industry and all its beauty and all its faults.

This means, in short, that the life of Jesus risen is handed on by every baptized layman. Each must be filled with immense joy and confidence at the signs of progress around him. We must not leave communists to spread alone the good news of a hope at the heart of history. Teilhard de Chardin has written: "Towards the peaks, shrouded in mist from our human eyes, whither the Cross beckons us, we rise by a path which is the way of universal progress. The royal road of the Cross is no more or less than the road of human endeavour supernaturally righted and prolonged."[1]

[1] *Le Milieu Divin*, op. cit., pp. 103-4.

Christ came to bring a more abundant life, and this life sprang out of death. This life is available now. It is a life beyond death and the touch of death. But we do not have to wait till after death before we can communicate in it. The resurrection order of life is precisely what we receive at baptism. In baptism we died the only death that matters and received the communication of the everlasting life won for us by Jesus. Joined to him henceforward we go out to the world to let it partake of his elevating and saving influence. For this world, like we ourselves, is not due for annihilation but for transformation. It is the place to which Christ will come from heaven when the last trump sounds.

The Bible never speaks of men "going to heaven". St Paul speaks rather, as we said, of Christ coming from heaven; but heaven is not "anywhere". Heaven is God; to be in heaven is to share God's life. To come from heaven is to bring God to the earth. This is what Christ did originally in his incarnation, and what he will do finally and perpetually when he comes in glory.

If heaven is not beyond the earth in any geographical sense we cannot show our belief in heaven by despising or disbelieving in the earth. There is a hatred of the earth, an unworldliness, which is profoundly unchristian, just as there is a love of the world to which only Christians hold the secret.

Conclusion

This chapter, entitled "Baptism in the World Today", has been an analysis of the Church. The Council's decrees have been quoted extensively to give the latest and most authoritative exposition of how the Church sees herself in these momentous times and how she conceives her role in the modern world. This was intended. Too often we look on baptism in an isolationist fashion, in terms of what is done to the individual soul, what graces and virtues he receives, how his sins are forgiven. My aim was to show the ecclesial effects and intent of baptism. God wants to save us in the Church which is his people and the very body of his beloved Son visible in the world until time ends. He wants, in other words, to save us not as individuals but together, through this social organism, the Church, and the social agencies of this organism, the sacraments. We are all bound together and gain strength in Christ and in the Church, the humblest little assistant in the draper's shop who bows her head and blushes at the wolf-whistles of the lads; enclosed monks and nuns, cellared like wine and waiting on God, arched and intently listening like squirrels in the woods at the snap of a twig; the pope himself with the burden of all the churches upon him. All have been baptized into the Church, and so all are priestly, prophetic and kingly. All are equally called to the building up of Christ's body. All are summoned to be apostles, to work for the more complete unity of the Church to which they belong, and to extend this Church and its saving message to the world around them.

IV

THE EUCHARIST IN SCRIPTURE

IN THE SECOND CHAPTER it was stated that baptism is not a sacrament which is over and done with on the day we receive it, that it has to be lived out in a whole lifetime, and that it is precisely in our reception of the Eucharist that we do this. Not only in the Eucharist, of course. We shall be coming to much the same conclusion in reference to the sacrament of penance. And it should not worry us that we keep coming back to the same point. We tend to split up the sacraments far too much, and to see them in isolation from each other. If these chapters can convey something of the unity of the sacramental system, and of the fact that they are all centred on the paschal mystery, it will do no harm. It is not a different reality which is being celebrated each time, but exactly the same one. The sacraments should not be presented as so many individual and independent aids to Christian living, least of all the Eucharist. They are all different expressions of the death and resurrection of Christ, without which they cannot be understood, again least of all the Eucharist.

To understand the meaning of Christ's death and resurrection, the chapter "Baptism in Scripture" referred to the Exodus. That reference needs to be opened out in this chapter. After all, our Lord celebrated the first Eucharist in the context of the Jewish Exodus anniversary celebration to suggest to us that this was the background which would best explain it to us. What did he mean?

The Exodus

Israel's Exodus out of Egypt in the thirteenth century B.C. was the most fundamental event in the whole of their history. It was *the* radical experience which was going to influence and shape the rest of their existence. It is quite impossible to exaggerate the importance of the Exodus.

Why? What had happened? Even on the material level one would class it as an event of the first magnitude, certainly for Israel. Without the Exodus there would never have been an Israel. Here was a rabble of displaced persons, enslaved, without unity, without a purpose, without a hope. Into that situation comes a leader who unites them, gives them a sense of purpose, brings them out of their degradation, guides them safely through a treacherous wilderness, leads them to victory over the numerous peoples that stood in their path, and finally gives them an identity and a land of their own. Even on a material level, on the level of plain history and of practical politics, such an event could never be wiped out from their memory. What had emerged from this experience was a people. This was the birth of the nation of Israel. It has been compared with the American War of Independence. No American history book, one imagines, will ever allow its readers to forget that event. No trueblooded American, one imagines, ever will.

But there is more to it than that. It was the Israelite prophets who pointed out that this was not merely a political experience, but a religious one. Because Egypt was not only the land of political slavery; it was also the land of idolatry and paganism. What Israel had been rescued from was not only bondage, but sin. And it was God who had done this, not for any merit or worth of theirs, but simply because he chose to. In a situation which was humanly speaking hopeless, when they were on the point of annihilation, when to all intents and purposes they were dead men, he had intervened to effect, as it were, this new creation out of their nothingness. It was, therefore, he who had led them through a watery grave into the hardships of the desert and there fed them to sustain them on their march to the kingdom he had in mind to give them. What Moses had proclaimed to them on that journey, therefore, was not simply a political constitution, a way of life to distinguish them from the nations round about, but the Word of God, by which God had committed himself to them, and had asked for their commitment in return. And when they did commit themselves, God had, as it were, become their husband, to whom they were now tied by a covenant which was a bond of marriage. God had become, as they called him, their redeemer, someone into whose possession they had passed, so that they could no longer call themselves their own but only the people of God, a nation of priests whose every activity was a kind of liturgy, a service of the God to whom they were dedicated. And it was God who had finally completed this laborious and painful transformation of theirs—this Exodus or transition from a life of slavery, idolatry, paganism and sin—by bringing them into the security and peace of Jerusalem, where he dwelt in their midst.

In the light of that prophetical explanation of the meaning of the Exodus, it is no surprise to find that, for ever after, the Israelites knew God as "he who brought us up from the land of Egypt". They realized that in this event he had shown them the basic shape of his plan for mankind, the permanent outline of how man, separated from God, is to be re-united to him. Man's redemption, his passing into the possession of God, would always have to be this sort of thing: an act of creation completely unmerited and undeserved, a rescue from godlessness and death, an acceptance of the Word of God whereby a covenant is forged, a journey, and an arrival at a kingdom where God dwells.

Clearly, what had happened in the thirteenth century B.C. was not the end of God's plan. This kind of experience would have to be lived over again many more times, each time at a deeper

level, before man's union with God could be said to be perfected. We find the Israelites particularly aware of this in the
sixth century B.C., when the Egypt-situation overtook them once
again in Babylonia, and they longed for another and more
fundamental Exodus to prepare them for a new Jerusalem.[1]
But it was not only once every few hundred years that they
became aware of this. They acknowledged it annually in their
celebration of the passover.

The passover

The twelfth chapter of Exodus lays down the ritual to be
observed at the passover meal, with the presumption that it will
be celebrated every year on the anniversary of the Exodus.
We call the ceremony a commemoration, a memorial service.
The word is accurate enough, as long as we understand it in the
way the Israelites did. For them, a memorial was not simply a
reminder, a souvenir, the kind of thing we might bring back
from Margate or Manchester to recall the delightful summer
holiday we spent there. In Hebrew, to commemorate is to
re-live something, to re-experience it, to renew it in the sense
of making it happen all over again. When they commemorated
the Exodus, they did not simply read or think about it, they
brought it into the present. That is why they made a meal of it,
so that they could eat the thing up and incorporate it into
themselves. A rubric still exists to make this quite explicit.
It reads: "In every generation, each Jew must consider that he
himself went forth from Egypt. It was not our ancestors alone
that the holy One redeemed. He also delivered us with them."[2]
To celebrate the passover was to be challenged to identify
yourself with the community which God rescued from Egypt
and bound to himself with a covenant at Sinai. To eat this meal
was to acknowledge that you could not be part of God's people

---

[1] See Isaiah 40–48, especially 41[14,18] 43[1–7, 16–21].

[2] Mishna, Pesachim 10[5].

unless you inserted yourself into this event, and acknowledged that this was the shape of God's plan for you too.

The shape of it but, as we saw above, not the fulness of it. What the Israelites were celebrating in this annual feast was not simply the past, but also the future. Just as the prophets had insisted that the first Exodus should make people look forward to a new one, so did the ceremony. The rabbis had a saying: "On this night Israel was saved; on this same night Israel will be saved." The ceremony was meant to make people stretch out their hands for that salvation. Indeed, many of the prayers make it quite explicit that future salvation was regarded as the fruit of the celebration. The rubrics even directed that there should always be one more cup than the number of guests. The spare one was for Elijah, the forerunner of the messianic days to come. Because those days to come, like the days gone by, were not something to daydream about at a distance. If the eating of the meal incorporated you into the Exodus of the past, it also incorporated you into the Exodus of the future. That also was, in a way, re-presented, brought into the present.

In short, to eat the passover was to identify yourself with the people of God, and therefore at the same time to recall the action by which God had transformed Israel in the past, to make yourself ready for the future transformation by which God would redeem Israel from *all* its iniquities, and to participate here and now in both.

Christ our passover

The message preached by the New Testament is called the Gospel because it is the good news that this hoped-for future has arrived. When the New Testament authors want to explain who Christ is and what he had come to do, they do so precisely in terms of the Exodus-passover theme. Christ, they say, is the new Moses who comes to complete what the first Moses left unfinished. What he proclaims on a mountain in Galilee is the new Law which brings to perfection the Law proclaimed on a mountain in Arabia. What he brings about is a new covenant between God and men, fulfilling everything that the Sinai covenant had been designed for. What he achieves is the final break-through of the new Israel into the new Jerusalem, which is the presence of God.

How? When and where did he do this? In his death and resurrection. His death and resurrection were precisely his "exodus"—that is the word used by the evangelist to describe what Moses and Elijah spoke about to him on the mount of transfiguration[1]—the laborious and painful process in which the barrier between men and God was broken, and this human body was transformed from the fleshly condition it shared with us into the glorified state from which it is able to pour out God's Spirit on all men. As both chapters on baptism tried to explain, it was our Lord's body which was to be the instrument of our salvation. But it could not be this until it had gone beyond its earthly condition. It is only in the resurrection that it received that fulness of life which made it the source of God's life to all men. The journey to God, the return to God's presence which all men longed for, took place first of all in Christ's body. When God raised the body of Jesus from the dead, the Exodus-passover which had first been outlined in the Israel of the thirteenth century B.C. was complete. And it was done on the anniversary of that first passover to tell us that this was so.

The Last Supper

That is the context in which we ought finally to try to understand the Eucharist. It was on the night before he died, when he knew that the hour had come for him to depart out of this world of the flesh in order to make the pass-over to his Father (John 13[1]), that Christ gathered his disciples together, took the bread and wine of the passover meal, and said: "I

[1] Luke 9[31].

have greatly desired to eat this passover with you" (Luke 22^{15}).

An outline of the Jewish passover may help us to appreciate how closely the Last Supper fits into its framework. For this annual celebration, these Easter duties of theirs, as it were, the Jews had first of all to make a pilgrimage to Jerusalem, as the only place—certainly in Christ's time—where the feast could be celebrated. There, each family had to take a lamb to the temple to have it officially sacrificed, so that its blood could be poured out on the altar. Their communion with that sacrifice consisted in taking the dead lamb home, and preparing it for a family meal on the evening of the feast. For this the best room had to be set out, with the table laid with water, wine, unleavened bread and lamps, and divans prepared for the guests. They were not going to sit for this meal, but recline. This was not a meal of necessity, the kind of snack they might take at other times, but a solemn and festive communion.

When the family arrived for the meal, they first washed their hands ceremonially, and then took up their position on the couches. The meal began with a cup of wine, which was announced as a symbol of the joy that this festival was meant to arouse in the guests. And then an hors d'oeuvres would be taken to stimulate the appetite for what was to follow. Everyone took a piece of lettuce and dipped it into a bowl of vinegar sauce on the table, and a second cup of wine was passed round to mark the conclusion of this first part of the meal. It was not till after that that the main course was brought in—the roast lamb of the temple sacrifice. And it was at this point, when everything was now on the table, that the youngest in the family had to ask the formal question: "What is the meaning of these various dishes?" And the father of the family had to re-tell the story of the Exodus.

The story was not told as a fixed formula: the father was left quite free to elaborate on the details as he wished. But he had to cover the essentials: that the lamb recalled and re-presented the animal which had been killed to distinguish the doorposts

of the chosen people, that the bitter lettuce re-created the
situation of bitter slavery in which they had then found themselves, that the unleavened bread re-presented the circumstances
in which they had escaped from slavery before the meal had had
time to rise, that the wine placed the family within the joy that
God's deliverance had brought to their forefathers. This free
elaboration of the Exodus story was greeted by the family with
the first two of the Hallel psalms, still sung every Sunday in our
own service of vespers:

> Praise, O servants of the Lord,
> praise the name of the Lord . . .
> who lifts up the lowly from the dust,
> and from the dungheap raises the poor
>
> (Ps. 113 (112)[1,7]).
>
> When Israel came forth from Egypt,
> Jacob's sons from an alien people,
> Judah became the Lord's temple,
> Israel became his kingdom (Ps. 114 (113)[1-2]).

As was suggested earlier, the joy expressed in these psalms
referred not only to something that had happened in the past,
but to something that was happening there and then. It was
there and then that the family was being inserted into that act
of God's salvation, and these songs of praise and thanksgiving
were an acknowledgment of the fact.

The main course of the meal began with the breaking of
bread. The father of the family would take the loaf in his hand,
and pronounce over it the *eucharist* or grace before meals:
"Praised be thou, O Lord, king of the universe, who dost cause
bread to come forth from the earth." Then he would break it,
and hand it round to each person at the table. After that the
roast lamb was passed round accompanied by the vegetables it
was eaten with, and the meal would end with a third cup of
wine. This was known as the cup of blessing because it took the
place of grace after meals. Its formula was another *eucharist* or
blessing of God for all he had done in the passover, beginning:
"Praised be thou, O Lord, king of the universe, who dost feed

the world with goodness, and hast given us a good and spacious land." It goes on to recall all the other blessings God has lavished on Israel, and concludes with a yearning for the last blessing of all, the new Jerusalem. That cup would then also be passed round to all at the table, and the celebration ended with the rest of the Hallel psalms being sung, the last being the Israelite *Te Deum*:

> Give thanks to the Lord for he is good,
> for his love is without end (Ps. 136 (135)²).

Even before the parallels have been drawn, we should be able to see that the Last Supper not only fits exactly into the framework of that meal, but in fact is that meal. The washing of the feet with which St John begins his account of the Supper (13⁴) corresponds to the ablutions with which the passover meal starts. The hors d'oeuvres corresponds to the remark on Judas's treachery recorded by all the evangelists: "One of you will betray me." "Is it me?" "It is the one who dips his food in the same dish with me."¹ The telling of the Exodus story would be done by Christ himself, as the president of the group: it was up to him to explain the meaning of the meal's various details. And it is as part of that ritual—not as something isolated or unheard of or out of the blue—that we are meant to understand the "words of consecration". It is as the first act of the main course that Christ takes bread, pronounces over it the *eucharist* or thanksgiving to God, and breaks it and hands it round to his disciples. The Gospel account of it is a kind of transcript of the passover rubric: "As they were eating, he took bread, said the blessing, broke it and gave it to them" (Mark 14²²). Similarly, it is as the conclusion of the whole meal (*postquam coenatum est*) that he takes the last cup of wine, again pronounces over it the *eucharist* or thanksgiving, and hands it round with the prescribed

---

¹ It would seem that Judas is not being specified by this phrase, but simply described as one of the table companions. It is not a remark which distinguishes him from the other eleven, but a comment on the enormity of his crime. Christ is going to be betrayed by one of these twelve intimate friends, who share the same food.

reference to the future Jerusalem: "Truly I say to you, I shall not drink again from the fruit of the vine until the day when I drink it new in the kingdom of God."

It is on these occasions that, just as he had said: "This lettuce is the bitterness of Egypt from which God rescued us", "This lamb is the sacrifice which marks the end of our slavery and the beginning of our freedom", so he says: "This bread which I break before you is my body broken in death"; "This cup which is about to be poured out for you is my blood poured out in death."

Now it may strike us as odd that the first Mass should have taken place within the complicated ritual of something else. We may feel that it diminishes the meaning of the blessed Eucharist to put it on a par with the rest of the ritual. We may feel that it loses all its point if it is *merely* a symbol, like the lettuce or the lamb.

If we feel that, we have not realized how much symbolism meant to the Hebrew mind. As we saw earlier, for them a symbol was never a "mere" symbol, a picture which only reminded them of something else. When a prophet made something into a symbol, it was regarded in all reality as forming part of what it symbolized. It did not remain what it was before. It was lifted above its ordinary significance and given a completely new value. When Ezekiel, for instance, made a model of a town, and attacked it and destroyed it, and said: "This is Jerusalem", that was not mere play-acting. From then on Jerusalem really was doomed to destruction, inevitably tied to this symbol with which it now formed one thing (Ezek. 4^{1-3}). When Moses poured out the blood of a lamb on the people and said: "This is the blood of the covenant which God makes with you", this was no mere symbol. The blood really effected the covenant-bond, because it had been raised to a new reality (Exod. 24^{3-8}). In the passover ritual, as we saw above, when the spokesman for God said: "This wine is our joy at being saved from slavery", "This lamb is the sacrifice which marks our freedom", he was not merely reminding his guests of the past; he was enabling them to have a real share in it. These symbols had become part of the reality of the Exodus, and to eat them was to participate in that reality.

And so it must be above all for Christ, the supreme prophet and spokesman for God. When he says: "This bread is my body, This wine is my blood", he is not simply saying: "This will remind you of them." He is giving them a real new value, lifting them to a new level of being, enabling those who eat them to have a real share in what he has made them symbols of. He is not simply representing that reality, but truly presenting it, making it present.

What is actually rendered present is best described under four heads:

1. CHRIST'S DEATH

The breaking of bread is already an eloquent symbol of a body broken in death. And wine is already a perfect symbol of blood, just as the chalice is a natural symbol of suffering. There is therefore no need to look any further for the symbolism, as if we needed both of them, separated from each other, to signify death. We don't. Either on its own would be a perfect symbol once it had been specified by the words of Christ. In other words, Christ is not saying: "Here is part of myself", "And here is the other part of myself." Each formula is complete in itself. "My body" means "my whole self, broken in death". "My blood" means "my whole lifeblood, poured out in death". The two consecrations were not, as in the Mass, set side by side to be contrasted with each other: there was a whole meal between the two. Each of them signified, and therefore made present, the death Christ was to die the next day.

2. CHRIST'S SACRIFICE

That death was not one which was to come to him un-expectedly and against his will. He was going to it quite deliberately. He wanted it to be an act of worship of God, a sacrifice he was going to offer. This is what we are meant to understand by the words: "My blood which is poured out for many" (Mark 14²⁴). It is a quotation from the book of Isaiah of the Suffering Servant, the one who pours out his life for the many in order to reconcile them to God (Isaiah 52¹³–53¹²). The idea is conveyed even more succinctly in St Paul's formula, which reads literally: "This is my body, which is for you", and can only be translated: "This is my body, your victim" (1 Cor. 11²⁴).

3. A COVENANT SACRIFICE

The sacrifice Christ referred to was not just any sacrifice. As he quoted the book of Isaiah, so he quotes the book of Exodus when he says: "This is my blood of the covenant", or "my covenant-blood". In Exodus, Moses had poured out blood in order to ratify a covenant which for ever after was to be the bedrock of the Israelite religion (Exod. 24⁸). Even so, the prophets from Jeremiah onwards had said that it was only a preparation for something more perfect. In the messianic age, God would make a new covenant with men, and what had happened at Sinai would be extended to all nations. It is in that covenant, they promised, that the passover theme would be completed, and men finally achieve their complete transition to God (Jer. 31³¹ᶠᶠ; Ezech. 34²⁵ᶠᶠ, 37²⁶; Isaiah 54⁹⁻¹⁰, 55³). That is what Christ is claiming to bring here. It is his death which is the sacrifice that ratifies the new covenant between God and men. That is the passover which completes and perfects the old. And this Supper anticipates it, and makes it already present.

4. AN ESCHATOLOGICAL COVENANT

Eschata means the last times, the times when God's plans are completed. All that we have been speaking of—death, sacrifice and covenant—is not merely one further stage in the fulfilment of God's plan. It is already in some way the final expression of it. We have already seen that Christ, in giving the chalice to his disciples, looked right beyond his death to the messianic age in its full reality, the kingdom where he would drink new wine; and that is heaven. His death brings that future age into the present, and marks the breaking in of that heavenly world into our own. And that too is anticipated in this Supper.

The passover of the Christian

What have we got, then, rendered present at this Supper? We have the death of Christ, which he freely accepts as a sacrifice, an act of worship of his Father in heaven. We have the final and definitive passover by which the distance between the world and God is bridged. We have the perfect covenant yearned for by the Old Testament, by which men are bound to God in an eternal bond. And we have the *eschata*, the last things, the glory of the new Jerusalem available here and now. "He who eats my flesh," St John reports Christ as saying, "has (now) eternal life" (6[54]). There is nothing more to be had, except the manifestation of it.

What we have got, in short, is the very saving act of Christ. This is what is being rendered present in this meal, so that those who eat it can have a share in that reality. It is just as it was with the passover meal, where the whole reality of the past, the Exodus, and the whole reality of the future, final salvation, was made available to those present, so that they could associate themselves with it. The disciples at the Last Supper shared in the very reality of Christ's saving act.

What, then, of those who were to come after, who were not present at this momentous meal? St Luke and St Paul, in recording the scene, have concluded it with Christ's command: "Do this in commemoration of me" (Luke 22[19]; 1 Cor. 11[24]). This reflects the conviction of the early Church that this thing, this Supper, this meal, had to remain, had to stand at the very centre of the Church's life if it was to continue to share in Christ's saving act. "Do this." Do what? Do what the disciples did at the Supper, and eat it. There was no point in just presenting it and staring at it. It had to be eaten so that it could be assimilated. It was like the passover, which no one could become part of unless he ate the meal. Christ could have given us his saving act in words alone, so that it could register on our ears and mind and memory. He chose to give it to us as food, to bring home to us the fact that we must receive it into ourselves as the very source of our life. As Fr McCabe puts it: "If I give you a cigarette or a new tie, I am giving you something that will please you, but when I pass you the potatoes I am giving you life. We *use* clothes and furniture and books, but we do not just use food, we are made out of food."[1] You and I are made of that body of Christ which achieved the definitive pass-over to God, that body of Christ which assumed our alienation from God in order to triumph over it, that body of Christ which is now filled with the life of God. It is in eating that that we accomplish our own passover.

But even eating it is not enough; we have to be in sympathy with it as well. Certain foods can do a person positive harm unless his system is geared to it. What we are eating here is a passing through death to life; we cannot do that meaningfully unless we are prepared to undergo the same experience. What we are joined to here is a body in a perpetual state of sacrifice, eternally immolated; we cannot associate ourselves with that if our own self-sacrifice is only spasmodic or non-existent. The life that is given us here is Christ's own risen life, his victory

---

[1] *The New Creation*, London, 1964, p. 73.

over sin and death (John 6⁵⁴); we cannot receive that if we are still in league with death.

This is, of course, the explanation of the strange liturgy of Maundy Thursday. On this day of all days, on this anniversary of that momentous Supper, we expect the readings to remind us at least of its institution, to comfort us at least with a description of this great gift. Instead we get an epistle which tells us off for our lack of charity (1 Cor. 11²⁰⁻³²), and a Gospel which reminds us of what Christ did before that Supper: he knelt down and washed his disciples' feet (John 13¹⁻¹⁵). Why? Because we are being told to go and do the same. This is what the Eucharist involves. "Do you see this act of self-sacrificing love," we are being asked, "this denying of self in order to be at the service of others? Well, if you are going to communicate in the Eucharist, it means that. I have given you an example. Now go and do likewise. Otherwise your communion will be a mockery" (see John 13¹⁵).

The person who is unwilling to do this, to die to himself in faith and love, to live in and for others as Christ did, has not understood what the Eucharist is about. "Lord I am not worthy", we say, and we are right, for so we are. But do we understand what it is that the Lord has done? "You call me Lord and Master," he says, "and you are right, for so I am, and you, therefore, are my servants" (John 13¹³). But "a servant is not greater than his master" (John 13¹⁶). "I, your Lord and Master, come among you as a servant, as one who serves" (Luke 22²⁷).

To do likewise, to become a servant like him, that is a painful and laborious business, as the Exodus was, as Christ's death and resurrection were. But this is our passover, and it is this that the Eucharist is supposed to effect in us. The Orthodox liturgy has a prayer to prepare the communicants for the Eucharist which runs: "Let us love one another, so that we can proclaim our faith in a God who is love." That is a very clear statement of the fact that the Eucharist unites us, indeed, to Christ, but to a

Christ who is the expression of what God is, which is self-giving love. We could put it another way by saying that what the Eucharist renders present is not only Christ but the Church, which is the community of all those who give themselves in love as Christ did. To belong to such a Christ and to such a Church involves a daily death to ourselves in order to be filled with the lifegiving Spirit of God.

So we come again to the same conclusion we reached in our consideration of baptism. We are reminded again that what we celebrate in these sacraments is not something different each time. It is always the same paschal mystery, the mystery of the journey we have to make in the Spirit of Christ to the Father. This is the mystery which the passover of Israel looked forward to, which the death and resurrection of Christ made available to us, and which we are able, in God's goodness, to live out in the sacraments.

V

THE EUCHARIST IN THE WORLD TODAY

THE DOCTRINE UPPERMOST in the minds of the first Christians was that of the coming or the presence of the Lord Jesus, the *Parousia* as it was called.[1] I suppose they would have thought it strange to call this coming a doctrine at all. That sounds so formal. They were just waiting for Jesus. He had been made Lord and Christ by his resurrection; he had ascended to his Father and sent the Holy Spirit so that he might be more closely joined to them. They were waiting for him to come back soon, to reveal himself soon, to manifest to them in a cataclysmic display his dominance over all the earth.

Surely he would not be long in coming. They strained their eyes to the heavens, more intently than the psalmist ever did. (Had not the angels said that Jesus would come in the same way as he was seen going into heaven?) You cannot concentrate too much if you want to catch a thief on the prowl in the night. If the coming of the Lord would be sudden like a thief in the night Christians would be ready. St Paul could say to them, "You are all sons of light and sons of the day; we are not of the night or of darkness" (1 Thess. 5[5]).

The first Christians prepared themselves for this coming by obeying the Gospel of our Lord Jesus (2 Thess. 1[8]). The unbelievers, the sinners, they knew, would "suffer the punishment of eternal destruction and exclusion from the presence of the Lord and from the glory of his might, when he comes on that day to be glorified in his saints" (1 Thess. 1[9-10]).

[1] Cf. Anthony Kenny, "Until He Come", *Clergy Review*, September, 1956.

Evidently, the actions of anybody who thinks that Jesus is soon to be "revealed from heaven with his mighty angels in flaming fire" (2 Thess. 1⁷) are *bound* to be affected. This coming underpins the whole of the Christian life. "Be watchful," says St Paul obviously referring to this coming, "stand firm in your faith, be courageous, be strong. Let all that you do be done in love" (1 Cor. 16¹³). They were not even to go on marrying and giving in marriage with the same kind of abandon as before. There may be an unexpected visitor at the marriage feast, the Lord Jesus. Would he not expect his brethren to be looking out for him rather than celebrating in a fashion that makes it seem as if he was never coming and that the generations were to continue endlessly? St Paul could write—even though he admitted he didn't know the exact day and hour of the *Parousia* —"I think that in view of the impending distress it is well for a person to remain as he is. Are you bound to a wife? Do not seek to be free. Are you free from a wife? Do not seek marriage. . . . I mean, brethren, the appointed time has grown very short; from now on, let those who have wives live as though they had none. . . . For the form of this world is passing away" (1 Cor. 7²⁶⁻³¹).

In the meanwhile the faithful had something to remind them of Jesus. Jesus, on the night before he died, himself gave them instructions about what to do. This was the thanksgiving over bread and wine (the Eucharist), the two-fold remembrance-sign of the Lord Jesus. And Paul adds after his account of the institution, "For as often as you eat this bread and drink the cup, you proclaim the Lord's death *until he comes*" (1 Cor. 11²⁶). To eat the bread, to drink the cup unworthily was a profanation of the body and blood of the Lord. It was for a man to eat and drink judgment upon himself. Many were guilty of this and St Paul tells them severely what the consequences of it have been. "That is why many of you are weak and ill, and some have died" (1 Cor. 11³⁰). He seems to mean that any one who judges himself truly escapes judgment: he receives the Lord's body and blood worthily. Such a one will be rewarded with a vision of the coming of the Lord Jesus, since he has fittingly celebrated this sacred rite which the Lord left to us as a reminder of him "until he comes".

In Paul's thought, then, it mattered little whether you prepared for the Eucharist or prepared for the coming, whether you judged yourself in relation to the Eucharist or in relation to the coming. The Eucharist, reminding us of Jesus, is a proclamation of Jesus' death, of his sacrifice in which we share by means of the effective symbol of eating and drinking. But because the Eucharist reminds us of Jesus it points to the future, too. It anticipates the time when he is to come not in ritual death but revealed with the glory which his death had won for him. For Christians, it was enough to know that if they were not unworthy of the Eucharist, they could face the coming with confidence and equanimity.

The synoptic Gospels record the words of Jesus at the Supper, which enable us to see why it was that Paul connected the Eucharist and the coming. After the institution of the Eucharist in the sacrificial terms of blood-shedding and covenant, Jesus says, "I tell you I shall not drink again of this fruit of the vine until that day when I drink it new with you in my Father's kingdom" (Matt. 26[29]). The sacrificial banquet on earth is a preparation for, and an anticipation of the feast in heaven. This day of the Lord's heavenly banquet is the same day of the Lord's coming of which Paul speaks.

But Jesus delayed. Years passed and still he had not come. Eyes scanned the heavens less hopefully, less intently. It was not only the unworthy who became weak and ill and who died. Even the apostles, faithful witnesses of the resurrection, were dying one by one. It was all very worrying. Paul's disciples must have felt he was quite literally guilty of a confidence trick. True, he hadn't given an exact date for the coming but he had given them a distinct impression. . . .

The Thessalonians were particularly anxious about their

dead. Was it that the dead had missed the central event of their Christian faith, the event for which they had prepared all their life long?

Paul was puzzled and made what, on the face of it, seems like the beginnings of a compromise. In reality, it is only that his attitude has somewhat softened. The living, he says, will have no priority over the dead, "The Lord himself will descend from heaven with a cry of command. . . . And the dead in Christ will rise first; then we who are alive, who are left, shall be caught up together with them in the clouds to meet the Lord in the air; and so we shall always be with the Lord" (1 Thess. 4[16–17]).

That was the important thing, to be always with the Lord. Then the time of the coming did not matter. What was the proof that we were not displeasing to the Lord, that God loved us? Surely it was the death of Jesus upon the cross. "For God has not destined us for wrath, but to obtain salvation through our Lord Jesus Christ, who died for us so that whether we wake or sleep we might live with him" (1 Thess. 5[9–10]).

In this very early passage, so much gentler than the strangely harsh judgment on the ill and the dead in 1 Corinthians—even allowing for the different context of the letters, the passages are difficult to harmonize—Paul is struggling for an insight into the real meaning of the Lord's coming and what its significance is for those who have been baptized into Jesus. It is not that the *Parousia* is ever to lose any of its importance for him: belief in that event was the summary and, as it were, the peak of the Christian message. But its proximity has not the consequence which at other times he seemed to credit it with, and certainly less consequence than his eager converts assumed. That Christ died for us is quite enough, he was telling them. Christians had all they needed to base their hope on when they reflected on that death. The Eucharist which proclaimed it was henceforth to grow more and more in stature.

In the later Gospel of St John, the judgment has lost a lot of its apocalyptic trappings and has become more spiritual. This is not to say it is any less real. Rather it is more real, more interior, more *present*. The judgment is now. Jesus says: "Now is the judgment of this world, now shall the ruler of this world be cast out; and I, when I am lifted up from the earth, will draw all men to myself" (John 12$^{31-2}$). For John, the judgment is connected with the death and the exaltation of Christ—the word "lifted up" is chosen deliberately so as to include at once and together the two notions of death and resurrection.

Once more we see why it was that the Eucharist was destined to be the focal point of Christian reflection. Judgment is seen in relation to Christ's death and resurrection, his passover. This passover event was, to use a phrase coined later, put under a sacrament by Jesus himself at the Last Supper. Jesus really does come in the Eucharist: there is a presence, a *Parousia* of the Lord Jesus. We receive him in a sacred meal which is the pledge of the heavenly meal. We are joined to him in a way that completes and deepens his presence in us, a presence which is already real by reason of faith and baptism. So intimate is this new eucharistic union that if we partake unworthily of the bread and the cup we profane Christ's own body and blood. We join ourselves as dead, as corpses, to the ever-living Christ. Baptism was a new birth, but by sin we have walked back into the world's grave, endeavouring to drag Christ there. We began to live again "according to the flesh" and are trying in communion to make ourselves one with Christ the life-giving Spirit.

The real presence of Christ in the Eucharist is for the sinner a condemnatory judgment. "Anyone who eats and drinks without discerning the body eats and drinks judgment upon himself" (1 Cor. 11^{29}). On the other hand, "if we judged ourselves truly, we should not be judged" (1 Cor. 11^{31}).

Today, because Christ has "delayed" his coming in glory, we tend almost exclusively to judge ourselves by reference to the Eucharist. Are we "ex-communicate" by sin or not? Are we unworthy to receive the body and blood of Christ or not? Are we ready to give a welcome to the eucharistic *Parousia* of

the Lord Jesus or not? The very wonderful hush and expectancy
at the consecration of the Mass evokes the kind of longing with
which the early Christians awaited the *Parousia*. In the West,
there is still the strong conviction that the highest form of
Christian *ascesis*, so much recommended by Christ and St Paul,
namely, celibacy, is required of the ministers who effect this
Parousia of Christ in the midst of his Church, and who prepare
this banquet for God's people as a pledge of the heavenly
banquet ahead.

Sacrum convivium

Let us develop the idea of the Eucharist as a banquet or
sacred meal. It was within the context of the Jewish passover
meal that Jesus instituted the sacrament. *"As they were eating,*
he took bread, and blessed and broke it, and gave it to them, and
said, Take; this is my body. And he took a cup, and when he
had given thanks he gave it to them, and they all drank of it"
(Mark 14[22-3]).

The Eucharist is a sacred commemorative meal. As the
Jewish paschal meal commemorated and joined the Jews to the
passover from Egypt to freedom, so the Christian paschal meal
commemorates Jesus in his act of passing from this world to the
Father, and joins us to him in that very passing.

Christ's flesh is real food. The bread and wine over which
Christ in his own person or through his ministers speaks those
sacred words really become his body and his blood even though
only faith can discern them there.

We must establish the primacy of faith in eucharistic devotion.
We can, after all, only truly feed on Christ's flesh through
loving faith, through the faith that baptism brings us. Without
faith, neither in the eucharistic meal nor outside it can we truly
feed on Christ in the scriptural sense.

Our sanctification consists in our union wth the sacred
humanity of Jesus Christ, the holy One of God, a union effected

by faith and love. Baptism initiated this union. We became mystically one with Christ in his body the Church. He became really present to us. The rest of our Christian life is an attempt to deepen that union with our saviour. Now Christ wished to enter into the closest possible union with us in the Eucharist. The heavenly and holy body of Christ enters into communion with us through our earthly act of eating. The aim is always a deeper spiritual or mystical conjunction with our Lord.

I hope I will not be misunderstood when I say that this reception, this eating of the Eucharist is a symbol of our possession of Christ and of our being possessed by him. I do not mean that the bread is *only* a symbol of his body: it is an effective symbol. What we receive is truly Christ's body and his blood. What I mean is that our act of eating is not an assimilation of Christ's body and blood in the same way as our consuming toast and coffee for breakfast is an assimilation of them. Christ, though he is present as he is, body, blood, soul and divinity, is not physically but sacramentally present in the Eucharist. This is why although our Lord insists that he is the bread of life, that the bread he gives is his flesh for the life of the world and that unless men eat his flesh and blood they cannot have life in them, he ends by saying: "It is the spirit that gives life, the flesh is of no avail; the words that I have spoken to you are spirit and life" (John 6[63]). The Eucharist is above all a sacramental and effective sign of our *spiritual* conjunction with Jesus who has been made "the Spirit" (2 Cor. 3[17]) by reason of his resurrection. It is a deepening of that union with him which was effected by faith initially and is deepened by faith continually.

Christ is in heaven, we are accustomed to say. But between heaven and earth there is no spatial distance. The Eucharist then is not meant to bridge—indeed, cannot bridge—any spatial distance between ourselves and Christ. To say that Christ is in heaven means that Christ is with his Father, belongs to the sphere of the divine. In the Eucharist, if we receive the bread and drink the cup with the discernment of faith, Christ takes us to himself more nearly. We are speaking of the nearness of persons, a matter, that is, of spiritual kinship, not of space-time. So nearly does Christ take us to himself that this physical act of consuming the bread and the fruit of the vine is now an effective sign of our spiritual intimacy with Jesus in his glorifying of the Father. What more tender sign of our closeness to him could our Lord have given us? Through this sign of eating we are made concorporate with Christ but not in any physicalist sense. We become, to use St Paul's words, *one spirit with the Lord*, one spirit with his spiritual and risen body.

To think of ourselves after receiving the Eucharist as tabernacles of Christ is really to miss the point altogether. The one thing a metal or wood tabernacle cannot do is commune with Christ: there is nothing more than the space-time relationships between physical objects. The Eucharist is, as we noted, essentially a deepening of an already present personal relationship between Christ and us. Already one with him in baptism, we become more and more one, one body with him, as husband and wife grow, as we say, more and more into each other in the course of their married life.

As the Eucharist presupposes faith and love for its effectiveness in us, so does it intensify the faith and love already there. It is, in this respect, not unlike ordinary personal intercommunion when the love we receive intensifies the love we are preparing to offer our friend. Our love feeds on the love we receive and grows stronger because of it.

One deeply ingrained tendency in human beings is to reify personal relationships, that is, in our minds to turn people into things and act towards them as such. We tend to want to tear apart the complex web of a person's thoughts, emotions, background and so on, and treat him as one of a category of people, as a number, perhaps. Categories and numbers are so much easier to deal with than individual flesh and blood. How angry we are when we find those we love are treated like this. It is a process not unlike that of a physicist who leaves aside all the vibrant, vivacious qualities of the world, sounds, odours, colours, to consider the quantitative aspects only, wavelengths, decibels and the like.

The tendency to reify, to materialize personal relationships, is not more evident anywhere than in religion. The result is an empty formalism, a ritualism gone through without the accompaniment of heart and feeling. It is really a return to the primitive in man, to the magical. We somehow fall a prey to the ancient and long discredited belief that objects have an effectual power in themselves independent of people and their personal response.

Even the sacraments are not free from such distortion. In fact, they would seem to be most susceptible to it, in that we know God has made the sacraments the instrumental and effective signs of his grace. In order not to debase the holiest elements in our religion, we have to tell ourselves repeatedly that the sacraments are not *things*, they are the actions of Christ. Since Christ personally intervenes by their means to save and sanctify us, our response, far from being dispensable, is absolutely vital. Even in the sacraments, God does not save us without us. The measure of our sanctification depends not on some pre-established parcel or quantum of grace which God is determined to give us regardless of our co-operation but on the quality and fervour of our response. The limit to God's graces is always put by us, not by God.

It is strange though true that we can even turn the Eucharist, the most alive and most personal relationship there is between ourselves and Christ, the point where we confront him most intimately as person to person, into a thing. The Eucharist then becomes *what* we receive into us. We are keener to "go to communion" regularly than we are to prepare ourselves for it worthily and to continue our "thanksgiving", which is what the sacrament is all about. We leave our Lord to do everything for us and in us. It is possible here as in the case of confession—

we hope that the possibility is not often verified—to receive the sacrament out of superstition, not out of faith at all.

To counter these tendencies it should be affirmed that it is not only consuming the host which is holy communion, but our co-operating to make of this consuming of the bread an effective sign of our spiritual communion with Christ. This is proven by what St Paul has said. Without faith and love the Eucharist is God's judgment on us. It is not a communion with Christ but perhaps the furthest departure from Christ that is possible in this life, not holy communion but an unholy separation.

If faith and love are needed for holy communion, they are not merely static predispositions. They are as well the tumultuous welcome we afford Christ. They are the music with which we gladden the feast.

Communion does not end with a worthy consuming of the host. This is only the beginning. In this the Eucharist is unlike normal food. Once we have eaten ordinary bread, we think no more about it: we leave everything to the biological forces of digestion and assimilation. Likewise, with ordinary medicine: we take it, hoping that the doctor or we ourselves have diagnosed the ill aright and prescribed the appropriate remedy; and wait for nature to resume its normal course. In both cases, it is a question of physiological determinism, of set patterns of cause and effect. There comes a stage when further intervention on our part becomes superfluous, perhaps even harmful.

Not so with the bread of life, the medicine of immortality. Here we need to co-operate at every moment. The actual consuming of the bread is only one stage of our conscious and responsible activity. That eating and drinking was intended by Christ to be the means of our communing with him on a higher level of love; and love is not a biological growth. Love is most intimately ours: it is ourselves. It is what we have freely, at every stage and at every moment, consented to become.

In one respect, of course, the Eucharist is like ordinary food:

its value is not completely determined at the very moment of eating and drinking. It is not sufficient that ordinary food should immediately sate our hunger or quench our thirst. The long term effects of some food that does that, we know to our cost, may be little short of disastrous. As the value of normal food is to be decided not at the moment of consumption but by its long-term effects on the bodily system, so the Eucharist does not exhaust its beneficial effects at the moment of reception. Afterwards we continue to benefit, to move higher up the ladder of love, as we have made plain, by freely co-operating with God's sacramental graces. Having forgotten the meaning of Eucharist as thanksgiving we think of what we call "our thanksgiving" as adjacent to, but not continuous with the Eucharistic celebration. This seems to me to be mistaken. This thanksgiving meal is not to be identified with the moment of eating, any more than the moment of sacrifice is to be exclusively identified with the two-fold consecration. The sacrificial meal is an affair of eating and drinking, and is not to be restricted—any more than is an ordinary meal—to the moment when we are actually putting the food in our mouths. The meal which is essentially a spiritual eating of Christ, a spiritual communing with him in worship of the Father, can go on for as long as the circumstances of our life allow. The aim in the forefront of our mind should be to prolong this particular meeting with Christ as long as possible and to take him with us into the world.

Eating together

We have until now spoken of the Eucharist as a sacred meal or banquet. It is of its nature a *communal* celebration as the word "communion" denotes. We not only commune with Christ, but because of him we are in communion with the Church, with the other members of our family.

A student of mine said to me recently that Joe Lyons and the cafeteria system in general has been considerably down-graded since the liturgical revival began. Liturgists are given to stressing the community aspects of meal-taking and denigrating the private, packaged lunch—those bits and pieces of food that you pile selectively on a tray and then proceed to balance like an acrobat as you walk across the crowded floor-space looking for a seat out of sight. Eventually you find one. You have to shift away the dirty plates and utensils and brush away the bread crumbs when you get there, but you now have a place to eat. You are not welcomed into any circle. You ask politely but briefly, pointing towards the greasy relics of the previous occupant: "Anybody's place?" or, "Is that taken?" If nobody objects or, better still, if there is a softly murmured: "It's free", you know it's yours. You appropriate it, as a pioneer might a strip of land, however temporarily. Then you proceed to eat, a stranger among strangers.

The liturgists surely have a point. How little fun there is in food taken among strangers or in strained and awkward silence. We all know the kind of experience referred to here. I would merely like to recall the memory by quoting from a couple of entries in my diary at a time when I was doing some research in a university city. Firstly, the initial acquaintance with the other lodgers in the boarding house where I stayed.

"This morning at breakfast. A doctor from Chile, an Italian, Rossi, from Florence and Mr Nikolaev, a Russian physicist. All combine charmingly to create perfectly and *really* what I had previously known only in caricature—was it a caricature?—the boarding-house atmosphere. So it's all quite true: the sound of strange tongues, the enduring and unendurable silences, the bits of conversation quite frenzied when they come but brief. Each sitting on his thoughts like a broody hen; but at the end becoming quite pally. Mrs F., the landlady, hovering over the stove in the stifling kitchen, cooking traditional bacon and egg with cornflakes as an hors d'oeuvre and marmalade and toast to follow. The foreigners—I was the only solid Englishman there, and even my ancestors come from Cork—were either exceedingly polite or not unappreciative of the hallowed English fare. They did not complain."

So much for the first meal in, now for the first meal out.

"The lunch out was inexpressible. The anonymity of everything; sitting at a table opposite someone who reads his paper while he eats, leaving you with little alternative but to do the same. The Semites with their convivial ideas of a meal together making you almost blood-brothers would not have made anything of this. The air in these restaurants must be sterilized of 'friend-germs'. People enter with the expression on their faces, 'I have come in here to eat. I shall eat quickly and methodically. Please leave me alone'. And they are left alone. The tables where people know each other and talk are like little oases in the desert. I almost feel they should have a palm tree growing up out of the centre of the table to mark the distinction of possessing the waters of human friendliness. The rest of us eat our meat and drink our milk and generally make the meal a business it was never meant to be—not entirely, anyway. . . ."

To receive the Eucharist is not simply to eat but to eat together. The Church our Mother feeds us with the body with which she is identified in a mystical marriage. She gives us the very body into which we have been incorporated by baptism. It was at baptism that the Church gave us faith to feed on Christ, especially in the Eucharist; and to feed on Christ is the very condition of being saved. The Eucharist is rightly thought of as the focal point of our faith, because without it there would be no Church in that there would be no Christ with whom the Church could be identified. Here we see the ecclesial aspect of the sacrament. Both the Church and the Eucharist are referred to as the body of Christ. The Eucharist makes the Church, just as in another sense the Church makes the Eucharist.

That Christ is given to us in the form of a meal is most appropriate since eating together signifies life together; and that is why to be excluded from a family meal is a sign of exclusion from the family's life. Eating together is the sign and proof of fellowship. (Hence the anger of the scribes and pharisees when Christ was discovered eating with the publicans and sinners. They were right in thinking that Jesus was openly proclaiming his friendship towards the fallen.) When someone shares his meal with us he is, as it were, giving us a share in his life. Food being the source of life represents life as given and received.

In the Eucharist Christ feeds us. Because bread represents life, he becomes the bread in order really and not merely symbolically to share his life with us. In giving himself to us as food Christ is telling us that he, and he alone, is the source of our life. That he is the life of us all as a community and not as individuals is what is represented in the meal. This would be even clearer to us if a single loaf were divided up among us and if we drank out of a single cup as obviously happened at the Last Supper according to Jewish custom. "Because there is one loaf," wrote St Paul to the Corinthians, "we who are many are one body, for we all partake of the same loaf" (1 Cor. 10^{17}). St Luke says of Jesus at the Supper: "He took a cup, and when he had given thanks he said, Take this, and divide it among yourselves" (Lk. 22^{17}). Hence the psalmist's lament fulfilled in Judas's betrayal of Jesus:

> Even my bosom friend in whom I trusted,
> who ate of my bread, has lifted his heel against me (Ps. 41^9)

Judas partook of the same loaf, a sign of friendship, and proceeded to hand Jesus over to the chief priests and the pharisees.

The eucharistic sacrifice

So far we have stressed the meal aspect of the Eucharist. Now we turn to the Eucharist's sacrificial character. "For as often as you eat this bread and drink the cup, you proclaim the Lord's death, until he comes" (1 Cor. 11^{26}). The Mass is here set out as a memorial of Christ's passion. It is not my intention here to recapitulate in any detail the teaching of the Council of

Trent on the eucharistic sacrifice. It is a theme that has, ever
since, dominated Catholic theology almost to the exclusion of
other important aspects. Even before the Reformation, in
mediaeval times, Christ's passion and death were at the centre
of the common folk's devotional life. When the Protestants
denied that the Mass was a sacrifice and affirmed it to be an
empty memorial, Trent reacted vigorously. Christ is truly
present whole and entire under the species, and under each part
of the species of the bread and wine. The Mass is truly Christ's
sacrifice. He renews on our altars the sacrifice of the cross.
He is still the priest offering himself, still the victim, in a
bloodless sacrifice of propitiation through the ministry of his
priests. Trent also lays down the principle that between Calvary
and the Mass the only difference is the manner of the
offering (*sola offerendi ratione diversa*). There could be no
clearer affirmation of the sacrificial nature of the Mass than
this.

Nevertheless, despite Trent's affirmation and the re-echoing
of it in theological manuals and popular catechisms, I have a
sneaking suspicion that the devotion of the people never fully
assimilated this notion of the Mass as a sacrifice. Naturally, they
asserted it in words. They could even express what were termed
the four ends of sacrifice, adoration, thanksgiving, reparation
and petition. However, their real approach may not have been
unlike that of a lady who recently gave us her idea of the Mass:
"It is the miracle of bread being changed into Christ so we can
worship him." The "miracle" is presumably the popular
expression of "transubstantiation". The notion that Mass is a
way of worshipping Christ—a longer and more elaborate form
of Benediction—is also still far from uncommon. As one book
puts it: "We can find the Mass numbered, by some excellent
spiritual authors, among the different means of honouring the
Eucharist."[1]

[1] Saint-Séverin, *The Mass, Christians Around the Altar*, London, 2nd edn. 1961.
p. 142.

I suggest that many Catholics have difficulty in appreciating the sacrificial aspect of the Mass because of a deeper maladjustment still in their devotional life. I am referring to the practical neglect of the doctrine of the Trinity.

Teachers sometimes ask, How is it possible to teach the difficult doctrine of the Trinity? The answer is that if the Bible is followed there is no difficulty at all. To show that this is the case, we have only to set out the basic elements of our faith as we might present them to children.

"When God made heaven and earth he created men and women to be his children. But people in the world were so disobedient and sinful they were not worthy to be called God's children any more. God the Father loved them all the same. He sent his only Son into the world. Jesus came and lived a life of obedience and love of his Father. He died on the cross to prove his love for his Father and for us whom he wished to be his brothers. If we are Christ's brothers we must be God's children again, mustn't we? We have Christ's Father for our Father. On the cross Jesus opened his arms wide to show he was offering himself and his life to his Father and that his love was so wide as to embrace all men everywhere. When he died, God his Father who loved him raised him from the dead by means of his Holy Spirit. When Jesus went back to his Father he sent upon his Church whom he loved as his wife his Holy Spirit in tongues of fire. The Holy Spirit is with us still, joining us more closely in our hearts to Jesus; and Jesus takes us and all our prayers with him to God the Father."

Jesus is God's Son and is worthy of worship. Is it not the case, however, that we tend to worship him *exclusively*? We have said enough about the role of Christ in our salvation and sanctification to show that we have no intention of minimizing our love for him. But by addressing all our prayers *to* Jesus, by forgetting, on the conscious level at least, the place of the Father and the Spirit in our devotions, we have lost the notion of Christ being our Mediator with the Father. This is why we tend to think of the Mass as a chance of worshipping Christ, instead of being the very sacrifice of Christ offered up to his Father in the Spirit for man's salvation.

It is worth examining the collects and prayers of the Mass, and the Canon, too, to see how the liturgy usually employs the following scheme: we pray to the Father, through the Son, in the Holy Spirit. Perhaps the most significant liturgical change, besides the words of consecration aloud, which could be made would be to revert to the ancient formula of the *Gloria Patri*. Before the Arian controversy it went: "Glory be to the Father through the Son in the Holy Spirit." It ensures a permanent Trinitarian form of prayer. It is a prayer-scheme perfectly adapted to the scheme of salvation which we just outlined for the teaching of children. It is the necessary theological basis for appreciating the Mass as the offering of his life made by Christ our Lord to God his Father.

It must be said that in a sense the Mass is more than the offering of Christ, unless we think of Christ in terms of the whole Christ, head and members. For the Mass is the sacramental offering of the Calvary sacrifice, and is, therefore, *the offering of all God's people*. It is the very heart of their religious service. Christ wanted, says Trent, to leave a visible sacrifice to his beloved bride, the Church. We said in a previous chapter that the whole people of God, the whole Church, is priestly. The Church is mystically made one with Christ the priest in his offering of himself to his Father. Never is she more one with him than in the eucharistic sacrifice. We are baptized into the body of Christ to be able to offer up this sacrifice of praise to God the Father.

Liturgical renewal

Since the Church is, of its very essence, a worshipping community, the liturgy "through which the work of our redemption is accomplished" must take first place in our lives. The liturgical renewal crowned by the Council's decree means that discussions about the fruits to be gathered in from public worship have ceased to be of mere academic interest, the exclusive domain of those bowed and reverend scholars who are accustomed to write books with more footnotes than text. They concern us all.

Since Christ is never so active or so effective as in the liturgy, the belated renewal of it is something to be marvelled at. Think of the liturgists who were labelled "cranks" when they campaigned for things which we are beginning however slowly and painfully to take for granted. What was once virgin island soil tentatively explored by liturgical castaways is in process of being trampled underfoot by countless trippers, hikers and campers. Pioneers must be prepared to suffer the same fate as the prophets.

Listen to this *cri de coeur* of Antonio Rosmini uttered as long ago as 1832:

> Surely if nations are capable of being healed, much more are the ills of the Church curable. It seems an insult to her divine Founder to imagine that he who prayed the eternal Father to make all his disciples, "one, even as I and the Father are one" (John 17[11]), would suffer a perpetual wall of separation to exist between the people and the clergy, so that all that is said and done in the celebration of the divine mysteries becomes unreal and meaningless; that he would permit the people for whom the Light of the World was born, and who were themselves born again for the worship of the Word, to assist at the greatest acts of his worship in no other capacity, so to speak, than that of the statues and pillars of the temple, deaf to the voice of their mother, the Church when in very solemn moments she addresses them or intercedes for them as her children: or that the priesthood, withdrawn from the people, on a height which is ambitious and

harmful because inacessible, should degenerate into an aristocracy, a peculiar society, severed from society in general, with its own interests, language, laws and customs![1]

The wall of separation between clergy and people is in process of demolition. The laity's involvement in liturgy *in church* is the necessary prerequisite of their apostolate *in the church*. In fact, they are not two things but one thing. The apostolate is extending the work of redemption, accomplished in the liturgy, into the world of daily living.

The Council has put the matter in theological fashion, in this way ensuring that the liturgical renewal is not like the fading flower of the field:

> Mother Church earnestly desires that all the faithful should be led to that full, conscious and active participation in liturgical celebrations which is demanded by the very nature of liturgy. Such participation by the Christian people as a "chosen race, a royal priesthood, a holy nation, a redeemed people" (1 Pet. 2[9]; cf. 2[4-5]), is their right and duty by reason of their baptism.
>
> In the restoration and promotion of the sacred liturgy, this full and active participation by all the people is the aim to be considered before all else; for *it is the primary and indispensable source from which the faithful are to derive the true Christian spirit* (Pius X); and therefore pastors of souls must zealously strive to achieve it, by means of the necessary instruction, in all their pastoral work (*Constitution on the Liturgy* §14).

The Church as a worshipping community

The Church is a community. She expresses what she is when the whole body is gathered for liturgical celebrations of which Christ is always the principal offerer. It is into this worshipping, believing community that the convert comes. It is the community that receives him, gives him faith, breaks to him the bread of the Lord's body, introduces him to the effective and saving Word of God. It is in the liturgy and especially at Mass that the unbeliever should be able to meet and bow the knee

---

[1] Cf. *The Five Wounds of the Church*, p. 25.

before the Lord Jesus. He should be able to meet him in the words and actions of worship.

We have at last established that the words should be intelligible to the community as a whole. "The word heard by all unites more easily than the word read by each."[1] A common language only unites if it is understood. When I tune in to Radio Netherland I do not feel particularly aggregated to the people of Holland, because I do not speak Dutch. Because they knew that the Latin tongue was not understood by the people, priests for the most part used to do them the courtesy of not letting them hear it. We Catholics who pride ourselves on having a sacramental religion of sacred signs—and words are the clearest signs there are—hitherto have had a liturgy of the deaf and dumb. Priests have often celebrated Mass as before a whole deaf and dumb community with a rather inexpressive sign language. I suppose we should be thankful that a high wooden partition was not erected to screen off the sanctuary as well.

Let us pursue the matter. We communicate with each other more by the ear than by the sense of sight. Deafness, we are told—and we do our best to imagine it—is an intense form of isolation. A deaf person cannot easily converse with his fellows, nor listen to the radio or television. The very aloneness of the deaf person came home to me when a young woman suffering from this affliction—she has been a cripple, too, for seventeen years, after a childhood accident—sent me this poem she had written called *In Silence*:

> Amid the clamour of this metal world
> The ceaseless sounds of strife—the mental stress
> I live alone in silence.
> To my brain—no more do come
> The myriad murmurs of this teeming life
> That once became my music.
> I have lost the magic of those moments
> When before I heard the restless world

---

[1] Saint Séverin, *The Mass*, op. cit., p. 133.

As blurred and background voices
Listening not—to catch the fulness
Of God's miracle of sound
Which now at last in vain I understand.
Lord, give me grace and strength
That though my ears are still
The mysteries of sight and taste
Of touch and smell appreciating
I may praise thee well
   And in my silence sing
   While patiently alone I do thy will.

What is most impressive about the poem is the sense of living alone in silence. This used to be what happened when Catholics came together to celebrate the Eucharist. For all their congregating they lived alone in silence. They were, therefore, more like an audience than a priestly congregation. Thank God, such days are ended.

Any word unites. A word is food that all can feed upon together. It is a communion. There are times when we whisper or speak words to individuals. Lovers, for example, who wish to be joined to each other in special bonds of communion fortunately do not let others listen to what they say. But there are times when people need to hear words as a group, as a community. The community is not composed of a lot of individuals *as individuals*, but individuals *as members of a group*. Take any meeting or congress. It is not composed of a lot of individuals listening to lectures, but a lot of individuals as a group listening to lectures. Were there only one person in the hall besides the lecturer, the latter's powers of communication would doubtless be diminished or desert him altogether. The experience of the speaker is modified by his audience, its size, its sympathies or antipathies. The experience of the listener is modified by his being a member of a body of listeners. It is important to see this reflectively. Although a group is made up of individuals they do not hear what is said to them as individuals but only in so far as they are affected by grouping. Men will commit themselves as a group when they would not do so as solitary individuals. They will act as a group when as individuals they would be afraid to.

While this is true of ordinary words and groupings of people, how much more true is it of God's Word and the assembly of God's people. God's Word unites. It is the food of life for all to feed upon. It is a holy communion, a *sacrum convivium*, like the Eucharist itself. There are times when we need to listen to God in silence, away from the crowd. Any attempt to discredit such a form of prayer is a sorry thing and against the clear teaching and example of Christ. But it is nonetheless God's Word publicly proclaimed that first united us to Christ in his Church, and we need constantly to return to the community which is built up on the Word of God, to the community which is the proper home of the Word. We have a duty to express publicly our faith in that Word, the faith that the Word brought us. We have a duty to express publicly our gratitude to that Word spoken in and by the Church, for that Word is a reconciling thing, and it justifies us and reconciles us to the Church we have injured by our sins. We are, also, a special grouping of people, a family, God's family. Our Father wants, sometimes at least, as does any father, to speak to all his children together. It really is his word that emerges from his mouth here and now. This is why it has the power to give faith to the unbelieving and to reconcile and save the sinner. It purifies us and makes us ready to receive the Word made flesh in the Eucharist.

We who hear the Word together as God's family accept a common responsibility towards it. We express this in joint words and actions. "To promote active participation," says the *Constitution on the Liturgy*, "the people should be encouraged to take part by means of acclamations, responses, psalmody, antiphons and hymns, as well as by actions, gestures and bodily attitudes. And at the proper times all should observe a reverent silence" (§30).

A true people's liturgy is still to be written. The actions— like the offertory procession—need to become more expressive.

We need more easily assimilable songs to bring the Mass to life on the human level. The song unites men—think of the Risorgimento with its patriotic and martial operas. It is also a form of teaching. The heretic Arius used to write "songs for the sea, and for the mill, and for the road, and then set them to suitable music."[1] Even today in mission territory the bible and the catechism must be put to song for the natives to be able to appreciate their message.

The Gregorian chant may suit a choir of Benedictine monks but it is scarcely satisfactory for a school Mass attended by youngsters who rave over the Beatles and the Rolling Stones. The Gregorian chant needs a high degree of sensitivity for its appreciation; and few possess it. It is of interest to record that the stand at the Earls Court Vocations Exhibition of June, 1965 which attracted most attention was manned by young seminarists with guitars. They provoked at least one youngster to say to a guitarist: "When I grow up I want to be a priest like you."

We must learn to sing as lustily as some of our fellow Christians. St Augustine said that "to sing is to love". St Cyril of Alexandria addressing Christ wrote:

> Sing to God the Father and make him known to me.
> Thy words will save me, Thy song will teach me.

Christ, the singer, is also spoken of by the Fathers as "the God of those who sing". Liturgical worship may be looked at figuratively as the harmony that the Church provides to the beautiful song of Christ. But this figure only has a valid application if song is itself a means of loving and expressing love. The Church needs her musicians, as she needs her poets, if what she teaches is to be prayed. Above all she needs music for the eucharistic banquet, for what banquet was ever complete without song?

In all these ways we have mentioned, words and gestures, songs and reverent silences, the community gathers its forces

---

[1] Quoted by Newman in *On Consulting the Faithful*, op. cit., p. 111.

together to express in liturgical, priestly prayer the love it has for God, a love borne on high to the almighty Father by its sanctified and exalted Lord. Here in the sacrificial eucharistic meal particularly, where men share in the one loaf of Christ's body, is the answer to the atomization of the larger society in which we live. It is for us in our schools and parishes to make this answer an evident one. If Christ is really true to his word, it is in the Christian assembly that he will be most easily found by men.

The Eucharist and the world

We have mentioned the apostolic character of the liturgy. In the Eucharist the Church possesses not only the source of her own unity, but the power to transform, to christen the world, to bring Christ's risen life to bear on all its problems.

I would like to suggest ways in which we should make the Eucharist more relevant to our times.

Feeding the hungry

The first suggestion begins with what may seem at first to be a digression.

What is the most astounding idea thrown up by modern technological advances? I should reply without hesitation: It is that for the first time in history all the hungry on earth can be fed. Christians should hate hunger with every fibre of their being. Wherever there is a child sobbing for food, Jesus is suffering. It is so easy to calm ourselves with the thought that that starving child will one day be replete at the heavenly banquet. Isn't that just the kind of lack of care which the communists lay at our door?

The earnings *per capita* of 80 per cent of the world's population is less than £170 a year. Mostly, earnings are under 100 dollars, including India where four to five hundred million people live. It is estimated, conservatively, that at least twenty-five million people die of starvation or as the result of under-nourishment each year. Not so long ago a White Father returned from the troubled land of Zambia sick and broken, having just buried seventy children in his parish who died for want of food. Millions do go hungry, and most are in Africa and the East where the final political shaping of the country is still to be determined.

The West became rich on the injustice of sweated labour, even that of young children, and on the inhuman confinement of factory and city life. Russia became rich through the demonic genius of Stalin who achieved in little more than a generation what the West took 150 years to accomplish. Millions died, especially the peasants when they resisted the collectivization of the farms. It was Stalin who transformed Marx from a questionably accurate political economist into an alarmingly successful prophet.

The poor of Africa and the East must be fed, without resort, we pray, to force or the imposition of ideologies. Only if the hungry are fed will war be averted. History shows that most wars have been caused not simply out of viciousness but out of need, because nations grow and need food and land for their people.

Gandhi once wrote:

> A starving man thinks first of satisfying his hunger before anything else. He will sell his liberty and all for the sake of getting a morsel of food. Such is the position of millions of the people of India. For them "liberty", "God" and all such words are merely letters put together without the slightest meaning. They jar upon them. If we want to give these people a sense of freedom we shall have to provide them with work. . . . Those therefore who bring them work and means of getting a crust of bread will be their deliverers and will be also the people who will make them hunger for liberty.

Gandhi knew at first hand the hungry millions "whose only God is their bread". We do not know it at first hand, but *we do know it.* If a naked, starving child appeared on our door-step we could not resist helping to the utmost of our powers. Today, the whole world is our doorstep. We know that hunger is a wrong crying to heaven for vengeance. We must listen and act.

The Church must teach us to listen, and show us how to act. She is the one whose task it is to teach men that God is their Father. How can her missions succeed unless she also feeds the hungry, for how can she teach someone who is starving to pray, "Our Father . . . give us this day our daily bread"? And yet even this miracle happens.

We must return to the Eucharist. What is the Eucharist but a matter of eating and drinking, of the hungry having their fill? Christ so loves us that he wants to feed us with his body and blood. And he himself is hungry in all his brethren everywhere. Shall we not feed him in our turn? We shall neglect his hunger at our peril, for he has told us that the Last Judgment will take the form of a social enquiry. "I was hungry and you gave me no food to eat. I was thirsty and you gave me nothing to drink."

If we examine St Paul's rebuke to those who make sacri-legious communions we see that this is the very context of his outburst. He was very angry because his converts were meeting, on the occasion of the Lord's Supper, in order to consume their evening meal. "In eating," he writes, "each one goes ahead with his own meal, and one is hungry and another is drunk. What! Do you not have houses to eat and drink in? Or do you despise the Church of God and humiliate those who have nothing? What shall I say to you? Shall I commend you in this? No, I will not" (1 Cor. 11$^{21-22}$). Then it is Paul goes on to speak of the first time Christ gave his own body and blood as food to his disciples, and to warn those who eat the bread and drink the cup unworthily.

Indeed, how is it possible for a Christian to partake of Christ and be unconcerned about the world's hunger? Shall we feast so well whilst others fast? Is not this to "humiliate those who have nothing"?

But what is the solution? At the local level it would seem that each parish could easily adopt a parish poorer than itself. This —or something like it—seems more than a mere recommendation, it is the command of the Lord. We have made poverty into a counsel and asked dedicated monks and nuns to practise it when poverty is an obligation laid on us all.

We can be good at dislodging burdens from our back. Take fasting. Our consciences are clear if we fast on Ash Wednesday, Good Friday and one or two other allegedly dismal days of the year, when we consume as much as an Indian might in a week. Take almsgiving for the missions. We feel satisfied with ourselves if only we put a ten shilling note in the eye-catching fez of a White Father when once a year or so he is allowed to beg in the local parish church.

Poverty, fasting, almsgiving—how the Old Testament and the New ring with the sound of them like big bells. Modern churchmen seem afraid of mentioning their names except on special and acceptably isolated occasions. So much fund-raising is for the parish's own augmentation or comfort. The fruit of the people's sacrifices goes to . . . the donors. I am convinced that even the poorest parish must give something away: the little widow parishes must give their mite. Christ gives himself to us, we must all give to him in return.

It is not enough for the individuals in a parish to be concerned for the poor if the parish itself, the Christian assembly at prayer, has no social concern. The parish represents and is a microcosm of the whole Church which is one with Christ in his immolation of himself for the world's salvation.

If the parish gives a lead in social action, if the priests take their preaching seriously enough to want to stir up social action, then there is no telling what effect there will be in the community at large. The love of Christ urges us on to tasks as yet unenvisaged and unknown.

Parochial almsgiving is not the solution to the hunger problem of the world. The less developed countries need more than food. The whole of economy needs to be stimulated. There is need of governmental action. We need only think of India with its teeming millions. To be really effective it has been estimated that Europe will need to give India over a five-year period £2,100,000,000. If this appears an extraordinarily large sum we must admit it is. It so happens that America gave to Europe in a four-year period after the war twice that amount. Remember that the population of India is twice to three times as big as the whole of Europe. Britain spends considerably more than the sum that India needs in any two years on tobacco alone. Moreover, £2,100,000,000 represents only one fifth of one per cent of the West's national income, which is growing all the time.

There is, then, a need of governmental action. But governments are made up not of Martians but of men. They are born and bred and educated and influenced here. It is for the Christian to be the leaven in the mass, to be, above all, the leaven of pity. Christians have a knack of making a noise about small moral issues and neglecting the larger ones. They neglect to make a noise about, or even to question, what seems to be an unprecedented moral unconcern. I am referring to rocket research, which the Oxfam magazine once cartooned as a space ship on its journey watched by huddled, hungry peasants. The mother is saying to her children: "You see, they're trying to find some underdeveloped areas."

Here is part of a review of *Watch This Space*, a book edited by A. P. Herbert[1]:

> For the next five years the Americans will be spending an average of about £60 a second on an effort to put a man on the moon within the decade. The overall budget is likely to exceed £10,000 million (almost five times as much as India needs for economic take-off in the same period) with an economic return which will be almost vanishingly small. The same sum could build 1,000 nuclear power stations, 600 channel tunnels, run the National Health Service until the middle of the next century (the text reads "until the middle of the next *year*", which is either a

[1] In *Discovery*, December, 1964.

misprint or unprecedented irony), build more than 3 million homes or feed 50 million people for 200 years (or feed the whole of India for a quarter of a century!).

As the reviewer, N. W. Pirie, remarks, "Traditionally the moon unsettles men's minds." Never before have we seen such world-wide lunacy.

Our parish collections are not going to solve the problems of the less developed nations. Private philanthropy is no substitute for the pursuit of public justice. But we can help to build up a body of public opinion that deprecates such wastage of resources when so many men, women and children are going hungry, and perhaps to channel some of the money into more creative forms of endeavour. The Eucharist, this sacrament of eating the Lord's body and drinking his blood, would suggest that at least we try.

The Eucharist out of Church

Another way of making the Eucharist relevant to our times has already been tried by the Church of England for some while with success and is now being tried by Catholics: it is to celebrate the sacrament where it is most needed—not in a nice ornate, hygienic church, but in the kitchen, or the parlour, or on the building site. The Bishop of Woolwich expounded this interesting idea in his essay "The House Church and the Parish Church", where he argued "that the only way to recover the integral connection of the Eucharist with daily work may be to take the whole thing back into the midst of the sweat and the muck it is meant to be offering and transforming."[1] As an adventure in the apostolate it is worth trying. There is no reason to consider this a gimmick. It is an attempt to let the common surroundings and the common utensils be seen as the holy things they are. Some of the reactions the bishop records are: "I now feel my house is really a bit of God's world"; "I can't just chuck my things around anyhow in this room now"; "We

[1] J. A. T. Robinson, *Essays on Being the Church in the World*, London, 1964, p. 89.

find we can't quarrel over the table on which the Holy Communion has been celebrated."[1] It does seem a pity, doesn't it, that only one building in the parish should be the site of Christ's redeeming sacrifice.

Conclusion

In this chapter we have seen that the Eucharist is the sacred meal of God's family. It is a meal which is also the Church's sacrifice offered to the Father for all the needs of the Church and the world. It is by reason of its form of eating and drinking a reminder of our obligation to feed the hungry and give drink to the thirsty.

If the celebration of the Eucharist is truly seen to be a community meal, a sharing in Christ's sacrifice, a means of expressing pity for the poor and the hungry, the local Christian communities will serve well the larger society of the world. And, in addition, they will have no reason for alarm when Jesus comes.

[1] *Ibid.*, p. 94.

VI

PENANCE IN SCRIPTURE

IN THE CHAPTER ON baptism in scripture it was stated that what "man in the flesh" needs, to rectify his relationship with God, is not a mere polish-up or improvement or upgrading. His situation is one which requires a complete transformation to make him right with God. This chapter will try to develop this thought a little, in reference to the virtue and sacrament of penance.

It was also stated that such a fundamental change was not something that man could work in his own regard, it had to be done for him by God; and that this is what happens at baptism, where God's plan of salvation, fulfilled for the first time in Christ's death and resurrection, becomes effective in each of us. Baptism is therefore a decisive moment on which there is no going back. It is an event which cannot be repeated. However, as we also saw, what baptism does for us and what it introduces us to cannot be totally achieved in one moment of time, as if we came away from the font confirmed in grace. That total transformation has to be lived out in a lifetime which is a constant turning away from sin. That idea also needs opening out in a further consideration of what sin is. What is our attitude to sin? What kind of reality do we conceive it to be?

Sin

If we ask ourselves what sin is, we can give plenty of actual examples: lying is a sin, stealing is a sin, adultery and hatred are sins. But if we ask what makes sin sinful, why these things are wrong, where exactly the malice lies, we reply in rather abstract terms of "an offence against God by any thought, word, deed or omission against the law of God". And in these legalistic terms the reality of sin does not really come home to us. As long as we think in terms of a law which must not be infringed, of an affront which can be got rid of by an apology, of an injustice which can be patched up by making reparation, of a debt which can be sorted out by payment—we are very far from the reality which God has made known to us by revelation.

How does scripture put it? In a far more concrete way. It is significant, to begin with, that the most usual word for sin in the Old Testament means "distortion". It is the language we ourselves use when we refer to people as "twisted" or "crooked". It presumes that there is a norm which is straight and true, and that this is something abnormal. The norm is God, the source of order, health, harmony and perfection—all that we include in the word "life". That is the good, and it is normal. Sin is that which endangers this norm, or corrupts it, or destroys it. And it is the act of a madman. It is significant that the Wisdom literature regularly calls sin "madness" and the sinner "a fool", someone twisted and sick and abnormal.

This already is helpful. It gives us a picture of a God who is life abundant, and of the kind of death-wish that sin is. But even this picture is too abstract. Scripture can be a lot more concrete than that when it wants to bring home to us the reality of sin. Think of a young man, says Christ, a teenager if you like, who finds life at home dull and irksome. So he leaves to set up on his own. At first he enjoys his new freedom, and spends the money his father has given him on everything that takes his fancy. But the money doesn't last for ever. He soon finds himself in difficulties, and eventually in such destitution that he has to sell himself, and become a slave in order to exist. And it is only then, in his utter hunger and misery, that he comes to himself and decides to go on the run and return home. And his father is waiting on the doorstep to welcome him back with tears (Luke 15¹¹⁻²⁴). That, said Christ, is a picture of what sin really is. It is not simply that what the boy had done was sinful. All sin, he said, is like that. All sin is leaving our Father's house; all sin is wasting the talents he has given us; all sin is selling ourselves into the slavery of someone who has no concern for us; all sin is turning our back on the Father who holds out his arms to us.

Or to take another example, this time not merely from a made-up story, but from life. About the year 750 B.C., at a time when a central Italian tribe were putting together the first stones of what they were later going to call Rome, there lived in Palestine a prophet called Hosea. A good man, his story in the bible begins with his marriage to a girl he loved dearly, called Gomer. They had three children together, but even before the last was born Hosea began to be very concerned over Gomer. She was spending less and less time at home, and the suspicion crossed Hosea's mind that she was not being as faithful as she ought. Eventually he discovered that she had made herself a common prostitute, and was living with any and every man who came her way. Finally she deserted him altogether, leaving him with his home empty, his children motherless, and his heart broken. For a time he thought that the only solution would be to disown her and so forget her. But it was no use. He still loved her and could not bring himself to drive her out of his thoughts. So he went in search of her, and even accepted the humiliation of paying off her lovers so that he could bring her home. And that is how they were re-united, with Hosea forgiving her everything and even planning a second honeymoon to reawaken her old love.

Now all this did not happen in secret. Hosea the prophet was well known, and everyone agreed that Gomer had been a bad lot to treat a fine husband like that. And that is when Hosea told them that this was also a picture of sin. He did not mean that Gomer's behaviour was sinful—of course it was, and everyone could see that. He meant that all sin was like Gomer's behaviour. What Gomer did to Hosea, each of us does to God when we sin. God is not merely a Father, he is a Lover, to whom our covenant with him has wedded us, so close is our relationship. When we turn our back on him to look for satisfaction elsewhere, it is a sort of adultery. We think we can forget God; he cannot forget us. He loves us with an everlasting love, even though it breaks his heart to do so (Hosea 1-3).

That, says scripture, is how we ought to think of sin. God is not someone who says: "You will do such and such or else." God is someone who says: "Look how much I love you; why do you keep leaving me, in your thoughts, in your words, and in your deeds." Sin is not simply an offence, a debt incurred, or an infringement of a by-law. Sin is the ingratitude of a child who turns his back on his father. Sin is the wantonness of a wife who turns up her nose at the love of her husband. Sin is a kind of league made with death, the negation of all the values which we put into the word "life". Sin would, if it could, bring back on to the whole of creation the chaos out of which God rescued it, in something of the way a horror-struck Jeremiah described a Palestine sunk in sin:

> I looked on the earth, and lo, it was waste and void;
> and to the heavens, and they had no light.
> I looked on the mountains, and lo, they were quaking,
> and all the hills moved to and fro.
> I looked, and lo, there was no man,
> and all the birds of the air had fled.
> I looked, and lo, the fruitful land was a desert,
> and all its cities were laid in ruins (Jer. 4$^{23-26}$).

Forgiveness

What is God's attitude to this reality that we call sin? The two parables quoted above have already suggested the answer. Humanly speaking, sin leaves a situation in which there is no glimmer of hope whatever. If it really is a kind of death, then there is no more reason to expect the situation to improve than there is to expect a corpse to get up on its legs. If it really is a

kind of broken marriage, then one could no more expect to get
rid of sin than one could expect a cuckolded husband to disregard or forget the brazen behaviour of his wife. Humanly
speaking, if we come across an example of grave sin—a thief
committing murder in the course of robbery, a father beating
his defenceless child black and blue, a tradesman swindling a
whole streetful of old-age pensioners—humanly speaking we
would use the word "unforgivable" of cases of this kind. And,
of course, if the matter happens to affect us personally it is even
worse. We find it hard enough to forgive an injury; the thing
rankles and we bear grudges for weeks. But what if some serious
crime is committed against us? A burglar finds the hiding-place
in which we have put our whole life's savings: could we ever
forgive that, or even forget it? And to think that all sins affect
God personally, that they are all committed against him! How
could he ever forget? If we reflected only on our sins, of thought
and word, of deed and omission, would we not be driven to
despair?

We would, if God were like us. We can only be grateful that
he is not. Winston Churchill coined a delightful phrase about a
rather stubborn and unrelenting parliamentary opponent of his:
"There but for the grace of God goes God." If God were like
us! "If you, O Lord, should mark our iniquities, Lord, who
would survive?" But no, "with the Lord is found forgiveness,
and plentiful redemption" (Ps. 130 (129)^{3,7}). He is the relentless
enemy of sin, but for the sinner he can only feel pity:

> How can I give you up, O Ephraim!
> How can I hand you over, O Israel! . . .
> My heart recoils within me,
> my compassion grows warm and tender,
> I will not execute my fierce anger . . .
> For I am God and not man . . .
> and I will not come to destroy (Hosea 11$^{8-9}$).
>
> My thoughts are not your thoughts,
> neither are your ways my ways (Isaiah 55^8).
>
> I desire not the death of the wicked,
> but that the wicked turn from his way and live (Ezek. 33^{11}).

He is what the psalmist says of him:

> He forgives you all your faults,
> and heals you of all your sickness . . .
> he crowns you with love and pity,
> he fills your life with good things. . . .
> The Lord is compassion and pity,
> slow to anger and full of love.
> His anger is not for ever,
> his wrath is not without end.
> He does not treat us as our sins deserve,
> or repay us according to our faults,
> for as high as heaven is above earth,
> so strong is his love for those who worship him,
> and as far as the east is from the west,
> so far does he remove our sins.
> Like a father pitying his children,
> the Lord pities those who worship him,
> for he knows what we are made of,
> he does not forget that we are dust (Ps. 103(102)³⁻¹⁴).

He is, as the Litany of Saints describes him, the *Deus cui proprium est parcere*, the God whose essence it is to forgive.

Nor is that fact simply proclaimed by a few texts. The whole history of Israel exists to announce it. It is a history which begins with an Adam whose claim for independence ends in his own slavery, but whom God forgives and promises to reinstate. And it continues with an Israel which lives the drama of Adam over and over again, showered with gifts from God, constantly squandering them to its own enslavement, and constantly being rescued by a God who is willing to forgive seventy times seven. The Flood, Abraham, the Exodus, the Judges, the Kings, the Exile, the Maccabees—what else is this but the story of a God who raises the dead to life, and whose forgiveness is far greater than man's capacity for sin?

And of course the New Testament proclaims exactly the same message. You and I, now, we might have imagined that someone as God-like as Jesus would give sinners a wide berth, that his holiness could not possibly tolerate any contact with them. That is certainly what Peter felt when he said: "Depart from me, Lord, I am a sinful man. You and I don't go together" (Luke 5[8]). But in actual fact we find not only that sinners are constantly flocking to him (Luke 19[10]), but that he is constantly seeking their company, to the extent that his enemies can sneer at him as "a friend of sinners" (Matt. 11[19]). When they brought him a sinner caught in the very act, someone whom everyone else was prepared to condemn, he said: "I don't condemn" (John 8[11]).

It was not that he was indifferent to sin: his very next words were: "Go, sin no more." In fact, the very opening page of the Gospel had shown him as the relentless enemy of Satan, with whom he would make no compromise (Matt. 4[1-11]). The constantly recurring scene of the curing of demoniacs shows him in the same light, as the strong man who robs Satan of his possessions (Matt. 12[29]). So, of course, do all his curing miracles, where what he cures men from is meant to be a picture of what sin does to man. There is even a text which describes him as groaning with anger at the deformation that sin has made out of man (Mark 1[41]).

But his anger is directed against the sin, not against the sinner whom he has come to rescue from this tyranny. For the sinner he has nothing but pity. "God sent the Son into the world, not to condemn the world, but that the world might be saved through him" (John 3[17], 12[47]). He was the shepherd who was willing to leave the rest of the sheep unprotected while he went in search of the one that had strayed (Luke 15[4]). He called himself the Good Shepherd who was willing to lay down his life for his sheep (John 10[15]). And when he finally did just that, his dying words were still: "Father, forgive them" (Luke 23[34]).

The New and the Old Testament revelations are absolutely consistent. If every sin is a kind of death which leaves us completely helpless and without hope, God is willing again and again to bring us back to life. Are there any conditions attached?

Conversion

The one condition laid down is what scripture calls "conversion" or "repentance". This is the call which rings throughout the two Testaments, from the prophets with their "Jerusalem, Jerusalem" down to John the Baptist and his "Do penance, for the kingdom of God is at hand". Our translation of the word is not particularly fortunate, since we have given such an odd twist to the word "penance". For us, "penance" is the annoying bit at the end, the Three Hail Marys or the Stations, which comes after we have been forgiven. Scripture supposes that this penance-conversion comes before forgiveness, because it is the turning away from sin without which no sin can be forgiven.

Why this should be so is obvious enough. It would be absurd to imagine the forgiving of a sinner which does not include his turning away from sin and back to God. Even God cannot forgive someone who does not want to be forgiven, or who does not admit that there is anything to be forgiven. To refuse to be pardoned leaves God's hands tied. The opening of ourselves to his forgiveness is obviously the indispensable condition of forgiveness.

But what this opening of ourselves, this conversion or repentance, consists in, is less obvious, and is open to many misconceptions. The thief who is caught by the police in a sense turns away from his sin in sorrow, but it is a sorrow for being found out. Give him a chance and he will probably be at it again. The employee who is given a job to do and makes a mess of it is sorry. But it is a sorrow for making a fool of himself. The child who is told off for being naughty has a kind of sorrow, and lets everyone know about it by going round looking miserable. But he is really only sorry for himself. None of these is what scripture means by conversion-repentance, because none of these measures up to the reality of sin. If sin is something more than an offence or a breaking of the law, if sin is a deformation and distortion of man as God made him, then conversion-repentance must involve a complete transformation. If sin is the destruction of a solemn covenant, then conversion-repentance must involve a new commitment and a renewed covenant. If sin is the breaking of a marriage-bond, then conversion-repentance must involve a return to the love that has been despised, neglected and betrayed. If sin is a sort of league with death, then conversion-repentance must involve an invasion of new life, a re-birth.

The Old Testament calls this conversion or repentance *shuv*, and it is a metaphor for going into reverse gear. *Shuv* is what you do to a field when you plough it: you turn it upside down. *Shuv* is what you do to a glove when you have got it on wrong: you turn it inside out. The New Testament word *metanoia* is less graphic because it is less concrete, but it implies a change which is just as radical. *Metanoia* means to turn your ideas inside out, to see things from an entirely new angle.

Far from being mere shame over the past, therefore, or regret over making a botch of things, or a turning in on oneself in self-torment—all of which is negative and quite sterile—repentance in scripture is something positive, a passing from one situation to another. To repent is not simply to admit one is on the wrong path and to stop. It is a dynamic thing, and involves turning round and moving away from death to the source of life. The word "conversion" hits it off perfectly. Everyone knows what an upheaval a convert has to go through; St Paul on the Damascus road is the classic example. Repentance is like that, without the dramatics. Isaiah gives a description of it:

> Wash yourselves, make yourselves clean,
> remove the evil of your doings from before my eyes,
> cease to do evil and learn to do good,
> seek justice and correct oppression. . . .
> Defend the fatherless and plead for the widow.
> Come now, let us reason together, says the Lord.

Though your sins are like scarlet they shall be white as snow,
though they are red like crimson they shall become like wool
(Isaiah 1[16-18]).

Or in the words of Christ:

Unless you be converted and become as little children,
you shall not enter into the kingdom of heaven (Matt. 18[3]).

In other words, conversion means to dispossess ourselves, to renounce our own powers and to become like a child—hungry, needy, dependent, and perfectly aware of it. Conversion means to renounce self, to take up the cross, and to follow Christ along the path he took (Matt. 10[38]). In short, to repent is to recognize Christ's own life and death as God's revelation of the only way in which we can reach him, and to commit ourselves to that. That is the reality of conversion, and it is the indispensable condition, the *sine qua non* of God's forgiveness.

Are we prepared to do this? Are we even capable of doing this? The short answer is, "No". This may shock some people, particularly those who are still infected with pharisaism. It is very difficult for us to get pharisaism entirely out of our system. But we only have to think back to the image of the corpse to see how true the answer is. There is nothing about a corpse which would entitle us to expect it to revive. If it ever shows any sign of life again, that can only come absolutely unsolicited from the God who alone raises the dead. If sin is a kind of death, then we are helpless not only as regards forgiveness but also as regards the conversion which is the condition of forgiveness. Not only are we unable to forgive ourselves, we cannot even repent to be ready for forgiveness. Both are a gift from God, and the right order is: "Convert us, O God, and *then* we shall be converted."

Nor should we imagine that this is a specifically New Testament doctrine. The prophets had realized it long before; the prophet, for instance, who prayed, realizing how weak and erratic his own heart was:

A new heart create for me, O God,
put a steadfast spirit within me (Ps. 51(50)[12]).

Or the prophet in Babylonian exile who stands aghast at the failure of his people to achieve their destiny, and looks forward to the time when they will allow God to do it for them:

> I will take you from the nations
> and gather you from all the countries,
> and bring you into your own land.
> I will sprinkle clean water upon you,
> and you shall be clean from all your uncleannesses,
> and from all your idols I will cleanse you.
> A new heart I will give you,
> and a new spirit I will put within you;
> and I will take out of your flesh the heart of stone
> and give you a heart of flesh.
> And I will put my spirit within you,
> and cause you to walk in my statutes. . . .
> And you shall be my people,
> and I will be your God (Ezek. 36[24-8]).

Or finally the prophet Jeremiah who, in the face of the same Babylonian tragedy, bitterly realizes that the kind of attachment which God asks of his people, which is not for anything that they would get out of it but simply for his own sake—this attachment would never be achieved by their own power. God alone could do it for them. The heart of man was too twisted. God must bring about a new creation and give him a new heart. Only in this way could God effect the new covenant with his people, when they had understood that all he wanted was their heart, however much it cost them. This was the proof that he had given them a new heart in exchange for their heart of stone.

> After Nebuchadrezzar king of Babylon had taken into exile from Jerusalem Jeconiah the son of Jehoiakim, king of Judah, together with the princes of Judah, the craftsmen and the smiths, and had brought them to Babylon, the Lord showed me this vision: Behold, two baskets of figs placed before the temple of the Lord. One basket had very good figs, like first-ripe figs, but the other basket had very bad figs, so bad that they could not be eaten. And the Lord said to me, "What do you see, Jeremiah?" I said, "Figs,

the good figs very good, and the bad figs very bad, so bad that
they cannot be eaten."

Then the word of the Lord came to me: "Thus says the Lord,
the God of Israel: Like these good figs, so will I regard as good
the exiles from Judah, whom I have sent away from this place to
the land of the Chaldeans.

I will set my eyes upon them for good,
and I will bring them back to this land.
I will build them up and not tear them down;
I will plant them and not uproot them.
I will give them a heart to know that I am the Lord;
and they shall be my people and I will be their God,
for they shall return to me with their whole heart" (Jer. 24$^{1-7}$).

The good news

It is the good news of the New Testament that the new
covenant longed for by Ezekiel and Jeremiah has come with
Jesus Christ. St Paul sums it up perfectly in the passage we
read as the epistle for Christmas day:

> We ourselves were once foolish, disobedient, led astray, slaves to
> various passions and pleasures, passing our days in malice and
> envy, hated by man and hating one another; but when the good-
> ness and loving kindness of God our saviour appeared, he saved
> us, not because of deeds done by us in righteousness, but in virtue
> of his own mercy, by the washing of regeneration and renewal
> in the Holy Spirit, which he poured out upon us richly through
> Jesus Christ our saviour, so that we might be justified by his
> grace and become heirs in hope of eternal life (Titus 3$^{3-7}$).

The new heart, the new spirit without which we could not even
begin to turn to God in repentance, was given us when the
Spirit of Christ was poured out into our hearts (Rom. 5^5).
Christ came precisely to give us his Spirit. It was the whole
purpose of his mission to give us the same relationship with the
Father which he had, and he was to do that by putting into our
hearts that same Spirit which united him to the Father. We
have already seen that he could not do this as long as he was in
the flesh. That condition of ours which he had assumed was a

barrier, a restriction, a hemming in of the Spirit which was his. It was only when he had taken his body through death, when he had died out on the flesh, as it were, that his glorified body could become what it was meant to be, the source of his own Spirit to us, so that the Spirit which converted him to the Father could convert us too.

This means that, even on this point, the New Testament message is a piece of good news. When Christ says: "Be converted, repent," he is not primarily waving a big stick at us. He is really telling us: "Accept this gift of conversion which is poured into your hearts by the Holy Spirit." Of course, to some it will sound like a threat. To the proud and self-satisfied that proclamation comes as a judgment. But we must realize that this judgment is itself an appeal to them not to close themselves to God's gift. The substance of the message is not bad news, but the good news that the union with God, which men could not achieve on their own merits, is given as a free gift; and that news is meant to fill them with joy. We have only to read the opening lines of the Gospel to convince ourselves of this: "Jesus came into Galilee preaching the good news of God, saying, The time is fulfilled, the kingdom of God is here; repent, therefore, and accept this Gospel" (Mark 1$^{14-15}$). When God has declared that a new world is breaking in on us, there is no more room for sitting on the fence. A decision has to be made, and it is one which cannot help filling us with joy.

This does not mean that nothing is demanded of us. If it is a decision, it is something we have to make for ourselves, and it is no easy or automatic decision. It may be easy to recognize that what one has been building so far is useless and worthless. But to pull it down, to demolish it completely, to begin building anew—that requires blood and sweat and tears. And that is what conversion is. Or, to go back to the image of Hosea, if conversion is the return of the unfaithful bride, then obviously the bride must play her part if the end result is to be a real love-match and not a mere *mariage de convenance*. When people are in love they are willing to go without food, or drink, or sleep, or anything that stands in the way of the one beloved. It is that sort of thing that the repentant sinner is required to do. If Christ's journey back to the Father involved a passion and death before there could be a resurrection, so does the repentant sinner's return, because as St Paul assures us his conversion is precisely a death and resurrection:

> All of us who have been baptized into Christ Jesus were baptized into his death . . . (And) if we have been united with him in a death like his, we shall certainly be united with him in a resurrection like his. We know that our old self was crucified with him so that the sinful body might be destroyed, and we might no longer be enslaved to sin. But if we have died with Christ, we believe that we shall also live with him. For we know that Christ being raised from the dead will never die again; death no longer has dominion over him. The death he died he died to sin, once for all, but the life he lives he lives to God. So you also must consider yourselves dead to sin and alive to God in Christ Jesus
>
> (Rom. 6$^{3-11}$).

However, that having been said, let it be repeated again that conversion is still a gift. This cannot be emphasized enough. What happens is not that *we* repent and so cause God to forgive, put him in a position where his hand is forced. What really happens is that *God* repents, that *he* relents. It is he who no longer holds our sins against us, he who turns us towards him to receive his forgiveness. God does not only forgive us, he makes us capable of forgiveness. Our repentance and his forgiveness are really two sides of the same coin, a gift from God. Of our own, off our own independent bat, we have nothing to offer. This must be emphasized. When we have recognized our sin and made the effort to rise from it, we cannot then pat ourselves on the back and bask in the sunshine of our own good conscience. Because what has happened is simply that God in his mercy has shone his light on us, himself revealed our sin to us, and himself moved us to return to him. Our return to God is indeed a painful one, and it requires our effort. But we have to accept even that effort as a gift from God. Repentance-conversion is always a raising from the dead, where we have nothing of our own to contribute. It is indeed we who do the rising, and a laborious business it is. But it is only God who does the raising.

The sacrament of penance

The reality of which we have been speaking throughout this chapter, this New Testament reality of repentance, conversion and forgiveness, is given to the Christian in the sacrament of baptism. This may be a surprising conclusion to reach in a chapter devoted to the sacrament of penance. But the fact is that for the New Testament it is baptism that is the type of conversion. Baptism was what the preachers of the Gospel were aiming at when they urged people to accept the good news and be converted. Converted for what? For baptism. Baptism was what they were thinking of when they recorded Christ's words to the apostles: "Whose sins you shall forgive, they are forgiven them" (John 20[23]). Forgiven how? In baptism. After all, we still admit the same when we say in the creed: "I acknowledge one baptism for the remission of sins"; and the same is presumed in our baptism ceremony, where the kind of thing we have been speaking of—the awareness of sin, the turning of our backs on it, the movement forward to God—is all supposed to have happened before the actual baptizing begins: "Do you renounce Satan?" "I do." "And all his works?" "I do." "And all his allurements?" "I do." "N. N. Will you be baptized?" "I will."

This has been rather obscured for us by the fact that nearly all our baptisms are infant ones. The reality we have been considering, this overwhelming conversion and forgiveness of sin, happened to us when we were unconscious. If we are ever going to realize it, that is, make it real to ourselves, we can only do it by living out our baptism in the sacrament of penance. All we can do is to try and see each confession as a kind of second baptism, and a much more laborious one than the first.

This does not mean that penance is a kind of substitute which we had to invent for ourselves once we began baptizing so early. Even in the primitive Church, adult baptism was never seen as the end of the affair. Even if the sacrament of penance had never been instituted, we would still have to live out our baptism in something like the way that penance tries to make us do. Because whatever the age we were baptized at, whether we were forty hours old or forty years, what happened to us then has to engage us at every level of our being, intellectual, volitional, emotional and social, and that cannot be done in a half-hour ceremony. It will take us the rest of our life. God's call to repentance and conversion comes to us not just once, but every day, and it is always a call away from sin. It is every day that we have to begin the journey afresh, as it were, to depart in order to make our pass-over to God. The whole of the Christian life is a penitential one, a dying to the flesh in order to be filled with the Spirit, because the whole of it is a constant conforming of ourselves to the death and resurrection of Christ. The process of being baptized "in water and the Spirit" (John 3[5]) will not be complete until we are totally glorified in the Spirit, after death. The doing of penance is a kind of daily rehearsal for death and resurrection.

Meanwhile we remain what Luther so well expressed, *simul justus et peccator*, at the same time justified and yet still caught up in the trammels of the unredeemed world, at the same time introduced into the new creation and yet bogged down in the flesh, and groaning with the rest of creation for the glorious freedom of the sons of God (Rom. 8[23]). It is because of that situation that St Paul keeps on repeating to his converts: "Be what you are! Realize what your baptism has made you—dead to sin and alive only to God. And then live out that reality in a way which indicates that you really believe what has happened to you." That is no easy task; it means, as Christ put it, shouldering the cross every day (Luke 9[23]). But it is not a doleful task either, because it is suffused with the light of Christ's Easter victory.

Something of what has been said here should influence the way in which we present the sacrament of penance. How exactly it is to be incorporated into our practice of frequent confession may be difficult to state: an attempt will be made in the next chapter. But clearly, if repentance-conversion is the kind of reality described here, it cannot be expressed as the routine chore or the formula we have often made of the sacrament. The kind of questions we must ask ourselves in order to make it into the constant conversion it is meant to be cannot remain at the old prayer-book level. They will have to be far more relevant to the reality we have been considering, and therefore framed more along the lines suggested by the Saint-Séverin community:

Fundamental Choices: Is my life lived according to the will of God? . . . Whom or what must I renounce today in order to fulfil God's will? . . . If I am already committed to a particular vocation or state of life, do I spend some time regularly (when and how long?) assessing my fidelity to it and estimating my progress? What still remains to be changed in my life?

General Questions: If God's will for each of us is a loving will, what response do I make to his love for me? . . . What do I do as regards my "religious instruction"? . . . How do I stand in my "religious practice"? Do I look on it merely as the fulfilment of a command or as an approach to the mystery of God? . . . Is the Mass, the assembly of the brethren round the Lord's table, the mainspring of my life? . . . What practical demands does my participation in our Lord's sacrifice make on my daily life? Am I conscious of an increase in fraternal charity from sharing in the holy Eucharist? . . . What do I do both in prayer and in my life for the missionary action of the Church? . . . What is my conduct towards non-Christians? . . . Do I pray for those without the faith? How much interest do I take in modern problems? What is my attitude to nationalism, colonialism, class-war? Is it in line with the teaching of the Gospel? . . . Am I aware of the living conditions of the greater part of the human race in the under-developed countries? . . . Do I look on all this as only the concern of specialists? . . .

Particular Questions: Money: Do I practise poverty in the Gospel sense of the word? Or do I live in order to make money and so get more comfort and enjoyment? What proportion of my means do I assign to the poor? . . . What relation does it bear to my personal expenses? . . . *Time:* What amount of time do I give to rest, recreation, prayer, work? to my family, friends and others? . . . Do I realize that prayer is, ultimately, an offering of one's time to God? . . . *Work:* Is it part of my spiritual life or just something quite apart from religion? . . . Do I make of it an offering to God? . . . Do I leave to others what is really my work, routine tasks in particular? . . . *Health:* Am I unduly afraid of suffering and illness? Do I make myself a burden to others? Am I prepared for death at this moment? . . . *Marriage:* How do I look on this state? As a purely secular one, easier than the monastic life, or as a form of consecration to God through the gift of oneself to one's partner and children? Do I consider my partner as . . . a means to self-indulgence, or as representing the love of God with all that it demands? . . . Do I look on children as . . . a token of God's blessing . . . a sign of his presence in my home? . . . Do I consider discord and strife . . . as a betrayal of God's love? . . . Do I look on my children's religious education as my primary duty? How do I carry it out, by word, example, the general atmosphere of the home? . . . *Celibacy:* Do I accept it in accordance with the spirit of evangelical poverty, for the love of Christ and the community? . . . Do I make use of my freedom from marriage . . . to be of service to others? . . . Or do I lead an aimless sort of life passed in vague dreaming, flirtations, melancholy, or all sorts of sentimental indulgence? . . . Do I devote as much time and care to the spiritual side of my preparation for marriage as I do to the material and social aspects? . . .

Do I give my life, in any sense? How? To what? To whom? Is it given in every aspect to God, to his love? Can I truly say, at this moment, before God, that I keep nothing at all for myself in my life, but, for love of him, I am ready to give all, according to the words of the Gospel: "If any man has a mind to come my way, let him renounce self and take up his cross, and follow me"?[1]

---

[1] Community of Saint-Séverin, *Confession, The Meaning and Practice of the Sacrament of Penance*, London, 1959, pp. 94–101.

VII

PENANCE IN THE WORLD TODAY

THE CURÉ OF ARS began one of his sermons with the words: "To talk to you about confession is to talk about all that is most precious in religion."[1] I firmly believe that this is the case. Whence comes, then, this strange uneasiness within me when I begin to approach the subject of penance in the world today?

It comes partly from the fact that I am not very happy with the present practice of confession among Catholics. The Council has decided that "the rite and formula for the sacrament of penance are to be revised so that they more clearly express both the nature and effects of the sacrament" (*Constitution on the Liturgy*, §72). When this is done there may be automatically a reversal of certain unhappy trends and attitudes in modern confessional practice.

Partly, my disturbance springs from the fear that nothing is so difficult to understand as the primacy of God in man's justification and subsequent holiness: there is always a tendency in us to become pharisaically self-righteous and it may, strangely enough, even be intensified by the sheer efforts we make to repent, unless we realize that even our best efforts at repentance are God's best graces. It is rather hard on poor, purblind mortals, isn't it, when their very attempts to tell God they are sorry for their sins may end in shipwreck.

Partly—in this case, I should say mostly—my unhappiness stems from my gross inability to understand many things which I would dearly love to understand, and which, I believe, I ought

---

[1] Quoted in Durrwell, *In the Redeeming Christ*, London, 1963, p. 79.

to understand at least better than I do. It should be stated from the start that despite my reservations about present customs of confessing, the plain fact is that many people find these customs profoundly satisfying and sanctifying. In the main, I shall be content to lay down the conditions for the most fruitful reception of the sacrament under the present discipline of the Church.

Those who need no repentance

Let me begin by illustrating how easy it is to misunderstand our condition before God. We shall examine the following well-known parable of Christ:

> Now the tax collectors and sinners were all drawing near to hear him. And the pharisees and the scribes murmured saying, "This man receives sinners and eats with them." So he told them this parable: "What man of you, having a hundred sheep, if he has lost one of them, does not leave the ninety-nine in the wilderness, and go after the one which is lost, until he finds it? And when he has found it, he lays it on his shoulders, rejoicing. And when he comes home, he calls together his friends and neighbours, saying to them, 'Rejoice with me, for I have found my sheep which was lost.' Even so, I tell you, there will be more joy in heaven over one sinner who repents than over ninety-nine righteous persons who need no repentance. Or what woman, having ten silver coins, if she loses one coin, does not light a lamp and sweep the house and seek diligently until she finds it? And when she has found it, she calls together her friends and neighbours, saying, 'Rejoice with me, for I have found the coin which I had lost.' Even so, I tell you, there is joy before the angels of God over one sinner who repents" (Luke 15$^{1-10}$).

A seminary student of mine was preaching not so long ago on this parable from St Luke. He spoke movingly of God's mercy following the sinner. How unlike, how much gentler than, man's mercy. He went on to illustrate Christ's meaning with examples of his own. How would we feel if we found ourselves sitting in church next to a man convicted of murder, to a woman of ill-repute, to a known Nazi war criminal? How would Jesus who sought after the one lost sheep have us feel about *these* lost sheep?

But the difficult sentence he completely overlooked, and so, I was convinced, missed the whole point of the parable: "I tell you, there will be more joy in heaven over one sinner who repents than over ninety-nine righteous persons who need no repentance." Why should there be more joy over one penitent than over ninety-nine just? Have we not been brought up from childhood to believe that innocence is better than repentance? Surely it is better to remain without sin than to sin and need forgiveness? Why, then, does Jesus say that heaven's joy is greater over the one repentant sinner?

Luke sees and tries to explain the difficulty. He goes out of his way to tell us that Christ's words are addressed to the pharisees and scribes who objected to Christ showing signs of friendship to publicans and sinners. The parable is evidently a piece of polemics. Most of Christ's parables have a cutting edge and this one is not less sharp than most. The clue to the correct interpretation of the parable, I suggest, is contained in the word "righteous" or "just". Jesus speaks of the ninety-nine righteous who need no repentance. In the context of polemics, by the "righteous" or the "just" Christ usually means the *self-righteous*, those who think they are doing God a favour by being good like the pharisee who figures in the famous parable with the humble publican. It was to such as these that Jesus spoke in intensest irony when he said: "I come to call sinners not the righteous." The ninety-nine righteous are, therefore, the self-righteous who claim to need no repentence, as the "sinners" are those whom the self-righteous may have written off but whom Christ pursues with his love.

The test is, How have we applied the parable to ourselves? Have we numbered ourselves among the ninety-nine sheep in the wilderness, among the nine silver coins safely lodged in the woman's purse? Or have we spotlighted ourselves as the lost sheep, the lost coin, found by God?

There can be no doubt about how we ought to think of ourselves: as lost and found. None of us is righteous of himself. We are all in need of repentance. We are all sinners, even if only some of us admit it. Paradoxically, we are *all* the one lost sheep, the one lost coin, whom God's merciful love has sought and found. It is the ninety-nine self-righteous who are left shepherdless in the wilderness, with a false sense of security, no doubt, from each other's company. It is the lost sheep who attracts the shepherd. It is the admission of sin that brings the saviour.

The student I referred to spoke splendidly of the generosity and extravagance of God's merciful love, but he forgot to mention, in this instance, that God's generosity and extravagance are only appreciated to the full when we see the copious force of it operating in our own lives. This only happens when we identify ourselves with the lost sheep.

Augustine wrote: "The beginning of all good works is the confession of our sinful works." The beginning of all holiness is the acknowledgment of our unholiness. Unfortunately, the pharisee, the self-righteous, is scarcely ever further away from us than half an inch below the level of consciousness. A saying of Rabbi Simeon ben Jochai goes: "Thirty just men, like Abraham our father, are worth more than the whole world put together. And if there were only thirty, I and my son would be among them. And if there were only twenty, I and my son would be among them. And if there were only two, those two would be me and my son. And if there was only *one* just man, that would be me."

We all need to experience what begins as blind terror and ends in sheer joy: that we cannot lift a finger to justify ourselves. We must bring home to ourselves that we are sinners—if we deny it, we are plain liars and the truth of God is not in us. And sinners are dead, as stone dead as Lazarus in the tomb. More exactly still, we are as dead as Jesus himself in the sepulchre: he lies there as the epitome of mankind's sinfulness, his godlessness, about which Jesus also cried out as he lay in agony on the cross.

If we acknowledge that we are dead, then God's Holy Spirit can come to justify us. Then we can emerge like Lazarus from the grave at the saving word of Christ. Then, most plenteously, do we share Christ's resurrection.

I have gone through all this because the sacrament of penance involves a true understanding of repentance to be fruitful. Some Catholics when told the Church's teaching on repentance simply do not recognize it as Catholic doctrine. So little do we understand the primacy of God's saving action in justifying us that we adopt an attitude almost exactly contrary to the one we should. We wait till we have by our own efforts "justified ourselves", and then go to confession to get God's seal of approval. I'm afraid that most of us most of the time spend our bouts of prayer trying like the pharisee to feel self-righteous. It is particularly dangerous when we know full well we have sinned grievously. We are like those people, spoken of by a character in *The Cocktail Party*, who cause harm:

> Because they are absorbed in the endless struggle
> To think well of themselves.[1]

That contrition is the very fruit of the sacrament, something given us by God when we confront him there, is something requiring constant meditation.

Present confessional practice

Having expressed my fear about our general inability to appreciate God's initial merciful approach to us in justification —the doctrine which Luther rightly saw to be the key to the New Testament—we must next turn to some doubts about confessional practice. I know no way of resolving some of them, and yet a clear and frank exposition of such doubts may have the effect of letting the deft mental fingers of others untie knots that my own nail-bitten brain cannot cope with.

[1] Act II.

I suppose all my doubts and difficulties are contained in sum in this one query: If confession does involve that which is most precious in religion, why is it that so many Catholics would characterize this sacrament, as "distasteful", "frightening", "a nuisance", and the like?

Why is it that this sacrament—and I am assured of this—keeps some people from friendliness towards God and familiarity with God?

But let us examine some of the difficulties in detail.

We are assured on all sides that sin is something social: it affects our relationship with God and our brethren simultaneously. This is why when we have gravely sinned we cannot receive the eucharistic body of Christ until we have been fully reconciled to the mystical body of Christ. Confession is meant to be a public acknowledgment of the harm we have done our brothers and a public reacceptance of us by the Church into full communion and fellowship. The Church who baptized us at the beginning baptizes us again, if need be, continually; and so we re-enter into the fullness of our priestly offices. But there is very little sign left of public reconciliation which penance—if true to the sacramentalism of the Church—should symbolize. A prie-dieu in a dark little cupboard; perhaps a screen or curtain to guarantee our anonymity for the absolving priest, the Church's minister; our satisfaction, a prayer for the most part, which only we the penitents are told of. This is all very secretive and unexpressive of our sorrow at offending our brothers.

What is very worrying about our present confessional practice is that it does seem to have taken the sacrament away from the hard-bitten sinners and bestowed the monopoly of it on those who need it less, and who, in fact, as we shall see, in some cases would even benefit from a lesser frequentation. Most confessions in public churches, if timed by a stop-watch, would probably be noted as lasting, on average, a minute and a half—give or take a few seconds. People with real sins, as they call

them, or real problems, might well hesitate to avail themselves
of an opportunity of implicitly parading their sins—not realizing
of course that this is precisely what the confession is, a sacred
parade of sinners! But they cannot be blamed for not wanting
to "own up" in public when no one else does. When the line of
penitents is going in and out like a weaver's shuttle, under-
standably they don't want to delay too long.

It is worth putting on record some of the things young
English girls have said about this. They appear in a most
interesting survey made by Sister Laurence, S.N.D., who has
kindly put her papers at my disposal.

One girl remarked, "I hate the stares people give you when
you come out after a long time." Another wrote: "I don't like
talking to the priest in the confessional because you have to
whisper in case anyone hears and when you come out all the
other people think you are some great sinner because you've
been in there so long." (It is a rather amusing thought that we
must conduct our confession in such a way that people will not
think we are a "great sinner". It does suggest what was noted
earlier, that many people go to confession unconvinced of their
sinfulness, a strange state of mind with which to approach the
sacrament of sinners.) A third girl said of the herd-confessions
of the school, "What will Sister say if I don't go and what will
the girls think if I am in a long time?"—an unhappy predicament, indeed.

I dare to say that there is a lack of seriousness about sin
betrayed in these remarks, in which, alas, we recognize too much
of ourselves for comfort. It is surely not the girls' fault: it is due
to the present swift confessional procedure. It appears very
often that they have more of a bad conscience about not going
to confession than about actually committing sin.

Father Charles Davis has written—I cannot accept the initial
statement unqualifiedly—as follows: "The effect of a Catholic
education on many is to pervert their sense of sin. An odd
statement to make, it might seem. Catholics are very much

preoccupied with sin, and Catholic children learn to classify sins with an accuracy that would have done credit to a moral theologian of a past age. But there precisely is the root of the trouble. The objective analysis of sin is not transferable to the subjective, personal judgment of conscience. Catholic educators do not take this enough into account."[1]

Well, *some* Catholic educators do not take it enough into account, if it is true, as we are told, that some penitents go on making the same childhood confessions right down "to decrepitude and silver hairs". The practice of what we referred to as herd-confessions in schools and which still prevails in many places is also of questionable value in developing a personal conviction of sin and enabling a child to confess sins other than those that teacher—in her innocence—has been able to think of. It is also worth pondering on just how many children who make fortnightly confession during the school term do not go at all in holiday time. This is the case even with adolescents who like to think of themselves as independent of school and parents.

Canon Drinkwater has campaigned more felicitously than I could hope to do, and longer than I would care to do, against confessions *en masse*. For instance, he wrote:

> While the practice of the Faith will not suffer from being associated with the corporate life of a Catholic school, it will suffer considerably from being associated with the drill and discipline of school life, as drill and discipline are often understood at present. . . . When we march them to confession in platoons and marshal them up to communion in companies, we are teaching them NOT to come to the sacraments. . . . What then? Some teachers are unable to perceive any possible mid-way between drill-religion and what they call "go-as-you-please"—the teacher must either have the children going to confession in ranks at his word of command, or else he must show no interest in their religious practices at all. . . . Children of all ages (and grown-ups, too, for that matter) need help; they cannot be left entirely to themselves in the sacred name of freedom; they need reminders, stimuli,

---

[1] *America*, 6 February, 1965, p. 193.

moral pressure, will-props of one kind and another. . . . What we propose is these props and pressures should be deliberately and progressively relaxed as the child grows older, so that his own will may get a chance to work. . . . We have to aim, not merely at the immediate formation of good habits in the hope that these may last, but rather at the formation of good habits which are *calculated* to last because they have taken root inside.[1]

The old campaigner ruefully remarks after these words that they were originally penned in 1918. May he have many medals pinned to his celestial chest.

Many further points could be made about the manner and frequency of children's confession and their age of initiation into this sacrament. I must content myself with these queries: If a priest as experienced as Canon Drinkwater questions the value of school confessions as true habit-forming—as opposed to the wrong sort of drilling—what *is* the value of them? Is it not strange that those who need the confessional least are made to use it most, starting from an age when even the greatest of child-haters—teachers, I mean!—would scarcely credit them with many opportunities for serious sins even if they could assume enough responsibility for them?

Moreover, under the present *isolationist* confessional practice, it can be quite a traumatic experience for children of seven whose lives are spent almost wholly in the company of others, especially of those with whom they have grown familiar.

The present confessional discipline of first confession before first communion can only be changed by the hierarchy. The Dutch bishops have already put off first confession to the age of eleven on the advice of their own catechists and child psychologists. But the present discipline has been in force for a long time: I find that it is as difficult to justify, as it is dangerous to attack. I am speaking of first confession as a general rule, because I believe that there are many children of the age of seven or thereabouts who would derive much benefit from the

---

[1] *The Sower*, April, 1965.

sacrament. They must never be deprived of the opportunity of making their confession should they so wish.

In these deliberations it should be remembered, to take a parallel instance, that when Pius X at the turn of the century changed the discipline of frequent communion every single book of moral theology had to be altered to fall into line. It was Pius X's decree on communion that caused the first massive increase in the number of confessions for venial sins; and recent mitigation of the eucharistic fast has added to them further.

Confessing venial sins

It would be well to voice some kind of doubts about the frequency, when it is conjoined with a lack of seriousness *in practice*, in confessing venial sins, however much one accepts theoretically the Church's teaching and discipline in the matter. We know that venial sin is not sin in the same sense as mortal sin. Mortal sin, by reason of its gravity, is in a way easier to understand as regards its effect, though its inmost essence—if one can use that word of what is really a privation or "non-being"—and its malice escape us. To commit mortal sin is to deny completely God's friendship: to commit venial sin is to act apart from God's friendship, to be forgetful and negligent of his friendship. In venial sin, we forgo doing what would make our love and esteem for God grow. It weakens our grip on God and so our preference for him above all things, which is what charity consists in. Notice, the preference for God remains. If it did not, then we would be without charity, the love of God would not be in us. But venial sin does not rid us of charity, though it hinders its exercise.

This also accounts for the difference in the pains of purgatory and hell, for purgatory consists in the purifying of our love, hell in the complete deprivation of love. To Madame la Comtesse, the Curé of Ambricourt said: "Hell is not to love any more, Madame. Not to love any more! That sounds quite ordinary to you. To a human being still alive, it means to love less or love elsewhere. To understand is still a way of loving. But suppose this faculty which seems so inseparably ours, of our very essence, should disappear! Oh, prodigy! To stop loving, to stop understanding—and yet to live."[1]

It is such love that mortal sin takes from us. It is only the grace of the sacrament that can restore it again. This is the primary reason why confession touches that which is most precious in religion: *it gives God back to us*. To speak in more personal terms, confession is God taking us back and clasping us to his heart with a love destined to last for ever.

But venial sin does not mean the loss of God's love, the emigration of the Spirit. We do not require confession to remit it. Under the influence of God's ordinary graces we make our act of contrition which is normal enough in that venial sin has not banished charity from us. All our religious duties and the offices of our state of life are directed, or can be, to the fostering of charity. There is no need to go to confession because of venial sins. The Council of Trent says explicitly that while venial sins may be lawfully and usefully mentioned in confession many other remedies can be applied to expiate them.[2]

Moreover, if we consider, as we have done already in the case of the Eucharist, what the apostles or the first Christians would have thought of our present confessional practice, we are forced to suppose they would have been somewhat surprised.

In the early Church it was not the custom to confess venial sin. Indeed, there is not a single document attesting such a practice. At first, penances were of a severe and public sort. Sinners were re-admitted to the community of the faithful, able to attend Mass and receive holy communion only after a penance that might last for several years. Should there be another fall, no further reconciliation was envisaged. It was not until the

---

[1] Georges Bernanos, *The Diary of A Country Priest*, London, 1965.
[2] *Denzinger* 899.

Middle Ages that confession of venial sins became a frequent occurrence, and it was only in 1215 at the Fourth Council of the Lateran that annual confession became the general rule.

These brief details from a complex history have been mentioned to show that the present discipline is not necessarily inflexible and, by the way, to indicate that ours is not the worst discipline imaginable by any means! The value of history is not simply to tell us of events and persons dead and gone but to cast light upon the present and the future. It is historical research which has made the present-day renewal of the Church possible: it has opened up the treasury of true traditions, allowed us to see that what we thought was genuine jewelry is sometimes only mediaeval or even Victorian bric-à-brac. This is not to say that what is oldest is necessarily the best. But it does allow us to discriminate better than we would have done and to determine where selectivity is possible, instead of having to take as gospel a development which took place as a result of misreading an authority in, say, 1763, or of a wild guess at what had happened until then in lieu of solid, historical scholarship.

In the case under discussion, it is pertinent to ask whether frequent confession does us very much good, which is the acid test of all religious rites: *sacramenta propter homines*. Is our detestation of our sins intensified by this means? Do we truly grow in the realization of our state of sinfulness before God, or is this eager haste to be "rid of our sins" a symptom of our inability to live with our sinfulness? Is the sacrament, as we make use of it, a real microcosm of our human condition as we hold out our arms to embrace the mercy of God: or do we reach such a state of boredom that we are delighted to find some fault or misdeed in ourselves not because it is an offence against God but because it gives us something to tell the priest? Do we go to confession to express our love for God or merely to clear our consciences? To quote Eliot once more:

> Your business is not to clear your conscience
> But to learn how to bear the burdens on your conscience.

What I am asking in short is, Do we use the sacrament of penance to intensify our sorrow or as a substitute for sorrow? If the latter, is this anything to do with the frequency with which we avail ourselves of the sacrament? And if it has, what is to be done about it? Each individual must answer these questions for himself.

I will suggest, later on, what is perhaps a more fruitful way of approaching the sacrament of penance. Even here, it seems relevant to remark that penance has suffered like the other sacraments—maybe more than the others—from being surrounded with an aura of magic. We were taught when young that perfect contrition—sorrow for sins because of offending God's love—justified us apart from confession. Imperfect contrition (or attrition)—sorrow for sins because of the fear of hell-fire—was not enough to remit sins of itself but was sufficient if, in addition, we received absolution from a priest. It was explicitly taught, in other words, that confession was a substitute for the more perfect form of sorrow, that God would justify the sinner without an inner transforming of his heart. No wonder that people so freely invested in a concern which promised such rosy returns without the heaviest kind of liabilities. Such a teaching would seem to imply also that the contrite, those who were more aware of sin because more aware of God's offended love, had less need of the sacrament. Those, on the other hand, with imperfect contrition who submitted to the Keys seemed merely to be fulfilling the juridical demand made upon them by a God intent on displaying to the Church the tidiness of the divine mind. There are other anomalies flowing from the teaching of an earlier generation. These, too, we will leave for a time until we proceed to something more positive.

Mortal sin and hell

I should like, however, to indulge myself with one last difficulty. It has to do with sin and hell. Father Charles Davis, in an article already referred to, criticized the announcement "that such and such a violation of Church law is a mortal sin". "Mortal sin" properly refers to formal, personal guilt. We ought rather to say that such and such a matter is of a serious nature, binding accordingly. "How sinful a violation will be depends on the individual's ability to evaluate the binding force of the law personally. To announce mortal sins is to commit a crude inaccuracy born of the disregard for the essential role of personal conscience."

Mortal sin, we said, is a complete denial of God's friendship, a basic preference of something creaturely to the creator. It is to cock a snook at God. At the judgment, it means that God will cock a snook at us.

Does it not do harm to proclaim unqualifiedly to infants that it is a mortal sin to miss Mass on Sundays, especially when they are told what the consequences of mortal sin are? Children are sons and daughters of their parents. The children of practising parents do not need such a threat: the children of non-practising parents probably won't heed it, or if they do, it is more likely to harm than help them. In all cases, then, the effect is baneful.

Think of the monumental problems facing a child of non-practising parents who endeavours to go to Sunday Mass. He has to get himself up on the only day in the week when his mother and father are still abed. With no alarm clock and little sense of time, with no encouragement before and no commendation after, he may have to make what for him is a considerable journey on a cold or rainy morning. When he arrives at Church he finds it peopled by adults: he feels he is a stranger.

These are the articulate thoughts of an adult on a child's predicament: what goes on unverbalized in the child's psyche is more hurtful still. It would appear morally indefensible to call it a mortal sin—which is a personally responsible condition entailing the personal punishment of hell—for such a child to miss Mass. Children in this instance are for the most part too dependent on their parents for the social and essentially family action of going to Mass to become their personal responsibility. As a result of the threat or even prospect of hell they may even grow up with a powerfully punitive super-ego, but this has nothing to do with Christain faith and Christian conscience about sin. The fear of punishment—the same is true of the actual receiving of punishment—can intensify the child's, and later the adult's, need to sin.

Psychologists and intelligent teachers have known this for a long time. J. A. C. Brown writes:

> It is, in fact, possible to transform a normal habit into a fixation by too much punishment. This is often seen in children who, when severely punished for some act, may have the compulsion to carry on doing it blindly. Maier concludes that punishment may have two quite different effects on the individual. Either it may have an effect opposite to that of reward and, as such, discourage the repetition of the act, or, by functioning as a frustrating agent, it may lead to fixation and the other symptoms of frustration as well. It follows that punishment is a dangerous tool, since it often has effects which are entirely the opposite of those desired.[1]

The aim of education is to impress good habits on children by love and not by fear. This also happens to be what the New Testament is all about. This is not to say that fear has no part to play in religion. It has as big a part to play in religion as in life under its other aspects. But it only performs this role when it is rationally and personally appropriated. The fear of hell which in the mature believer "is laid like a bridle on our hearts" (St John Chrysostom), is not necessarily belief in it any more than the fear of hobgoblins in the dark means that they are believed in. What is dangerous about a too vivid and too anxious early acquaintance with hell is that it gives to a child a distorted picture of God, thus making it easier for him when an adult to disbelieve in God altogether. With the dismissal in later life of the myth of a God who punishes with hell-fire a child of seven

---

[1] *The Social Psychology of Industry*, Penguin Books, London, 1954, pp. 253-4.

for missing Mass, the whole system of religious values may disintegrate.

What has beeen said of infants applies *mutatis mutandis* to the adolescents with their problems of sexual awakenings. These, also, can be too simply and too globally categorized as mortal sins. Take the instance of a young lad who finds pleasure in his own body simply, at first, as a physical discovery. It may be a quite new and unprepared-for experience. What begins as a mere biological happening he is told, without any nice distinctions, is a mortal sin. (This in its clumsiness is rather like telling a child that a hospital is a place where men in white overalls cut people's limbs off—and nothing else: a ludicrously unsubtle kind of characterization of a hospital and hardly calculated to prepare a person to go there should the need arise.) Such a piece of information does not help him to cope with a problem which from the biological standpoint is only a matter of adult maturation. Fear of committing grave sin and liability to hell-fire is more conducive to causing fixation in this instance than in most. For the boy cannot prove his sincere intention to be good by running away from temptation as is possible with most other sins. He cannot run away from himself. He is left puzzled and afraid. He feels, perhaps, soiled and besotted with sex. The fierce picture of God he conjures up for himself, on the basis of things he has been taught, may mean that never in his lifetime afterwards does he feel a complete trust in and kinship towards God. He knows not of anyone who would be as cruel towards him as God is thought to be.

Youngsters are also taught—and this makes matters worse—that not to reveal mortal sins in confession is a sacrilege. Yet is it not evident that the failure to confess what they believe are serious faults is due not to any lack of love but to a lack of nerve? They haven't the courage. They are not irrepressible sinners intent on telling a lie to the Holy Ghost—what a terrible thing that would be—but only timid children who don't know how to express what they consider they have done wrong, and are too embarrassed to tell it to a stranger anyway.

This is a human problem: it arises only in the case of confession and not in any other sacrament. The graces of penance are given as a result of this interpersonal relationship of a most unusual sort between priest and penitent. Any defect in the priest's personality or approach can cause a defect in the acts of the penitent which form the very matter of the sacrament. A fear of, or a lack of rapport towards the priest may induce a penitent not to confess his sins. This may seem hard to believe, in that withholding a serious sin in confession is designated a sacrilege. The fact that it does happen shows very well that the fear of direct consequences will not help a person overcome his natural reluctance to confess his sins. It will only give him a very bad conscience.

How are we sure that children conceal their sins in confession? It is the most important finding of Sister Laurence's survey which I mentioned earlier. Let us once more quote the verbatim reports of the girls.

"At the moment I am troubled with a sin, a very grievous one, which I will never dare to tell a priest, I don't think, but countless times I have confessed it to God in the privacy of my room." Another wrote: "When I have had a bad problem . . . thinking the priest wouldn't understand, I haven't told it in confession." Here is what others said: "When in there (the box), I feel too guilty to say what I really want to say and so just rattle off the usual sins." "I do not confess *all* my sins mostly out of shame and embarrassment. I do *not* feel guilty or the least bit wrong about this." "I seem to go through the same sins every time, but quite often I have some sin that I wouldn't tell the priest because I don't think he'd understand." "I do not always tell the priest the truth for fear he would recognize me." "Sometimes I don't know how to tell the priest my sins so I don't tell him at all." "When I examine my conscience thoroughly I come across sins I would be too scared to tell the priest . . . so I use the list I was given years ago."

It is probable that children who find it impossible to speak of their serious problems in confession experience this sacrament as something that cuts them off from Christ rather than as something that unites them to him. Far from being a means, it becomes a barrier to a fully heart-felt forgiveness. This makes plain on new grounds that the frequency of confession is not necessarily a gauge of its effectiveness.

There are many abuses of the sacrament, as is the case with people who think that once they have committed grave sin they might as well commit several, since going to confession is a distasteful business anyway, and, besides, "might as well be hanged for a sheep as for a lamb". There are many poignant misunderstandings as in the case of those who think that only actual confession can rid them of their serious sins: so that they suffer agonies of mind in the interim period, feeling apart from God, unworthy and unclean. I would like very much to dwell on these problems as on others such as those that beset the scrupulous. But the time of testing and probing is ended. It is time to build.

God's merciful love shown in confession

"To talk to you about confession is to talk about all that is most precious in religion." Nothing should shake our conviction of this. Confession tells us of God's continuing love for us and his ever-present mercy.

> The Lord is compassion and love,
> slow to anger and rich in mercy. . . .
> For as the heavens are high above the earth
> so strong is his love for those who fear him,
> As far as the east is from the west
> so far does he remove our sins.
> As a father has compassion on his sons,
> the Lord has pity on those who fear him;
> for he knows of what we are made,
> he remembers that we are dust (Ps. 103 (102)[8-14]).

Confession is a matter of God's judgment on us, but it is a judgment of justification not of condemnation, provided that we truly judge ourselves and accept God's merciful pardon. When we offend a friend grievously, he it is who holds the secret of forgiveness. Likewise, when we offend God, it is his alone to grant forgiveness.

We will examine the sacrament of penance in the light of God's fatherly and compassionate love, on the one hand, and man's waywardness in sinning, on the other.

A man baptized died to sin as surely as Christ died on the cross. He was received into the community of salvation called the Church. The Church is Christ's body vivified by Christ's own Spirit; and because of the Spirit this body is knit together in love.

After baptism, iniquity has passed but infirmity remains, says St Augustine. Man is ever in danger of being sold to sin again by the traitor within the walls of his own flesh. A piece of wire once bent can be bent back again to its original shape, but the bias remains in it: it is not twisted any more but it is weaker than it was. So it is after sins committed and forgiven: iniquity passes, infirmity remains.

Sin is not to love God above all things. The condition of never more being able to love God above all things we call hell. Sin is also not to love our neighbour with a genuine love. The condition of never more being able to love our neighbour we call hell.

The love of God and the love of our neighbour for God's sake are one love not two. Just as God does not love himself and us *as well* but he loves us in the one love he has for himself, so in divine charity, which is our share in the love God has for himself, we love our neighbour in the love we have for God.

It is enough for us to examine our love for our neighbour to know if we love God. This saves us the tremendous and terrible anguish of knowing if we really do love the God we cannot see.

Loving God above all things

Nonetheless, although the test and trial of our love of God is the love of our neighbour, what is it to love God? Charity is said to be the love of God for his own sake because he is the highest, quintessential Good. To love God is to take complacency in his goodness, to prefer him before everything else in the world.

Is not this most difficult to do? Of course, without God's grace, it is impossible, but it is not abnormal. Far from being abnormal, *it is the very condition of salvation*. To be in charity is precisely to love God for his own sake and above all things. How could a man be saved if he loved something more than God? This latter is precisely what mortal sin consists in. From the beginners who crawl around in the cellar of the seven storey mansion to the saints on the summit of mystical mountains, we must all love God above everything else.

The proof of our love of God is our love of our neighbour who is everyman. To hate anyone is to hate God. To love or hate anyone is to love or hate Christ, God's Son, who in mystical fashion has identified himself with everyman and become thereby the fount and the focal point of the unity of the Church and of the brotherhood of the whole human race.

That loving our neighbour is sufficient and necessary proof of loving God is too evident from scripture to need much elaboration. We Christians do not have to keep to the ritual of Leviticus: St Paul says, "He who loves his neighbour has fulfilled the law" (Rom. 13[8]). He is not of God "who does not love his brother" (1 John 3[10]). "We know that we have passed over (i.e. are joined to Christ's passover) from death to life, because we love the brethren" (1 John 3[14]). To love the brethren is to live out our baptism. It is enough to know we have forgiven our brethren to know that our Father in heaven has forgiven us all our sins. The Last Judgment is going to be a social enquiry: Have we loved our brethren? Then we shall possess the kingdom.

Have we failed to love our brethren? Then we shall go into eternal fire (cf. Matt. 25).

If we fall out of love with God, we fall out of love with our neighbours, too. In life, if we injure a neighbour, it is not enough to tell God we are sorry: we must ask our brother's forgiveness. If necessary we must leave our gift before the altar to do so. We who are baptized into Christ's body, have been baptized into a body of love. So closely knit together is this body that "if one member suffers, all suffer together" (1 Cor. 12²⁶). If we, by serious sin, wound the body we must plead forgiveness of the whole body. It is the body of Christ, the Church, who forgives in Christ's name; and so we know that God forgives us, too. But we must be truly sorry for our offences. Unless we are, we are still not in love: we are still dead limbs in a living body. We are still a scandal and an offence to our brothers.

Contrition and attrition

What sort of sorrow is required of us? It is customary, we noted, to distinguish attrition from contrition because the motives are different: by attrition we are sorry because we fear the pains of hell, by contrition we are sorry because we have offended God's love. It is commonly thought that attrition with confession is sufficient to justify us. This, I should say, cannot be maintained.

To be sorry because we are afraid of the pains of hell is not truly to repent at all. Fear of punishment is not the same as sorrow for the *guilt* incurred and has not of itself any saving value. True repentance must at least involve sorrow for the *guilt* of sin. A man to be justified must also *turn away* from his sin, and he can only do this if he loves God above all things. This is simply to say there is no true repentance without contrition, and to be contrite a man must hate his sin and love God, with the love of charity, above all things.

Naturally, if one makes charity too difficult, contrition becomes too difficult as well. But we have seen that charity is not something abnormal but the very normal condition of salvation; and God is always prepared to give us its grace, if only we are prepared to accept it.

The grace to be truly contrite is a sacramental grace, a grace which comes to us through the sacred sign of reconciliation which Christ left to his Church. Our contrition itself is given us through the community. It is, apart from our own personal efforts, the community's gift to us and acceptance of us. This sets the seal on the Church as the community of reconciliation into which we entered initially at baptism. She who celebrates the sacrifice of reconciliation continually calls us sinners back to sharing in that sacrifice by letting us eat the Lord's body.

To claim that the grace of contrition is a sacramental grace does not contradict what I said earlier, namely, that a man's sins are forgiven immediately he is contrite even before there is uttered over him the sacramental absolution. His contrition involves an implicit desire for penance. Or, rather, penance is operative in his very desire. To understand this, we need only think of the ancient patriarchs who were saved by their faith in the Christ who was to come and who had not then come. It was *Christ* who saved them. He was at work already in their desire. So it is with the Church's sacrament of forgiveness and reconciliation to the fellowship of love.

Since true contrition demands charity, without which no one is justified, attrition is not enough for justification, even though the sacramental absolution is added for good measure. But it so happens that the actual absolution is designed especially to raise the acts of the penitent which begin perhaps as imperfect to a higher level of sorrow. The sacrament's task is to give the grace of contrition. If the sacrament has not bestowed it before the penitent steps into the box, it may bestow it in the box itself, or even afterwards when the penitent is inspired to some act of love. Confession, therefore, makes one who was only attrite into someone contrite. If there were no inner transformation of the penitent, the sacrament would be simply a juridical process instead of "a making holy". It would be a substitute for the penitent's acts instead of a means of remaking his heart. St Thomas Aquinas never wavered in his belief that actual sin is not forgiven without an actual movement of contrition. It was the substitution theory which encouraged as did nothing else the idea of the sacrament working by magic. In the concrete situation, it would appear that most people who go to confession are truly contrite in that they do love God above all things. This is equivalent to saying that what many modern theologians call "attrition" earlier theologians called "contrition". Aquinas, for example, insisted that contrition was needed for justification and claimed that if the penitent had not already fulfilled what is necessary for justification, the actual reception of the sacrament normally gives him the grace to do so. Of course, the penitent may not respond. In that instance, the confession has not benefited him at all.

The place of love in penance

It is important to stress that the sacrament is under the sway of love. "The sorrow of contrition," says Aquinas, "is caused by charity." Only love can compensate for a love that has hitherto been denied. We see this first of all in the case of Christ who repaired the harm caused by our sins. He did so by expressing in his life and death a love for God greater than was the detestation of God shown in man's sin. His love like ours was two-fold. He went to his death to show the world how much he loved his Father and to give the greatest possible proof of his love for men.

Satisfaction is showing forth the love which was once denied. Christ became one with us, became sin *for our sakes*. This is why his crucifixion is our great act of contrition. Christ wanted to die to manifest in his death his love for God whom our sins had offended. He became sin and then died to sin. The Father received this immense act of love and because of it forgave us all our sins. This is why Christ's death is our hope of forgiveness. This is why in baptism and penance we are plunged into that death.

It is not always appreciated that the work of redemption is wholly a work of love. It is so often presented as a piece of vindictive justice, though there is no scriptural basis for this at all. In so far as there is any pain in the crucifixion it is man's work: in so far as it is the expression of love it is the work of God. God's love and man's sin meet in the body of the Crucified.

Let us follow the course of events in their historical unfolding.

When we sinned, God in his kindness prepared for, and finally sent his Son. Christ does not give at any time the impression that he is paying back to God just claims for damages. He is all love for his Father: he is assured that his Father loves him, that his Father's love never leaves him. And all his life's work including the cross is bathed in this love. The wole thing is a matter of the restoration of a broken friendship, not of a treaty made between two enemies or a debtor bargaining with a creditor in any legalistic fashion. It was, after all, *because the Father loved us* that he sent his Son into the world, sent him to share at first our alienation from himself but only so that his Son should be able to express in his mortal condition his perfect love for his Father. In this way, Christ went to glory, taking us with him.

These reflections enable us to see what satisfaction for sin must mean for each of us. In personal terms, it is for me to show God now the love I once refused him. It is to try now by my acts of mortification and by my life to love him far more than once I loved the world. By sinning I turned to creatures and away from God: by mortification I share anew in Christ's death to sin and the world in order to participate more fully in his resurrection life. Never is there any suspicion of paying God back according to the measure of strictest justice; rather, it is the reconciliation of friends. Love is the prevailing motif. The very essence of contrition and satisfaction is that a man is united to God by charity. We are sorry because we love, and since we love we cannot do enough to make up to him and to express our sorrow in word and action for having offended him.

I want to give one last important example to bring out the primacy of love in our relations with God. St Thomas says that if a person scrutinizes himself, examines his conscience, and overlooks a mortal sin which he has committed, and if, subsequently, he goes to communion with devotion "he does not sin; rather instead, by force of the sacrament (of the Eucharist) he obtains the remission of his sins".[1] He obtains through the Eucharist the grace of charity which brings about contrition and the remission of sins.

Two important lessons follow from this. Firstly, we need never worry about supposed mortal sins committed in the past which may have escaped our memory. Many people, unfortunately, do have such worries. A strange idea underlies them— the idea that God is less merciful than men and is liable to punish them for things which they have long forgotten even though their lives are subsequently blameless. It is wrong, too, on another score: the Eucharist is a sacrament for the remission of sins and will remit any forgotten sins by giving us the grace of charity.

The second lesson is this: if we have a genuine doubt about whether we have committed mortal sin and whether there is need to confess it before reception we should not refrain from holy communion. Rather, let us take the opposite course. If we receive with devotion, the sin will certainly be remitted by the grace of the Eucharist which makes us truly contrite. The grace of the Eucharist is the grace of love, and love is what unites us to God.

---

[1] 4 *Sent.* d. 9a.3 q. 2.

Suggestions for making a fruitful confession

I want to conclude this chapter by suggesting ways in which our confession can become a more fruitful experience.

We need, firstly, to realize that confession epitomizes our condition before God. We play the part of Nathan to ourselves, accusing ourselves of our sins so that God will, in his mercy, overlook them. We assume with joy the rich role of the publican, and beat our breast while saying to God: "Lord, be merciful to me a sinner."

We must remember, too, that penance expresses our contrition before the Church whom we have injured by our sins. To sin is to offend our brothers. There cannot be true contrition unless there is this, at least implicit, intention of submitting ourselves to the Keys of the Church. It is this intention that gives to our repentance its sacramental value The Church is a forgiving and reconciling Mother, and confession tells us of our need for her and increases correspondingly our love for her.

Confession will be appreciated further when we reflect on how well it follows the pattern of the incarnation. God did not simply tell us we were forgiven. He sent his Son to *express* his love and pity and forgiveness in Christ's passover. God wants to express his forgiveness in each individual case. This is why we have individual baptisms and individual confessions.

Confession must be looked at above all as a meeting with Christ. In this sacrament we meet him, as it were, in his most forgiving mood. It would make the sacrament more real and effective if we thought of it more in terms of going to communion. This is not so strange, After all, there is a sense in which we approach the Eucharist as we would the sacrament of penance. Do we not say three times "Lord, I am not worthy" before we receive the body of the Lord? What is there to prevent us approaching confession as we would the sacred table? The aim of both sacraments—as of all the others—is a closer union with our Mediator, Christ. It is in his merits that we trust, not in our own. There is no better reminder of this than in the sacrament of penance.

Since we realize that penance is not what happens in the confessional and is not simply the priest's absolution, we should do our best to make our confession a complete *celebration*. In religious houses, on the days when the confessor comes, some brief communal gathering might be arranged. A short service could easily be devised, consisting of readings from scripture and a public expression of sorrow for sins committed.

Where this is not possible each individual should still endeavour to solemnize his confession. Preparations could begin with the morning's Mass, the sacrifice of reparation. The whole of the day could be dedicated to reflecting on our condition as sinners before the all holy God. This is not meant to be a morbid pre-occupation with our iniquities. We should think more of God than of ourselves. Nonetheless, the recognition of our sinful state is, for the Christian, not a subject of occasional meditation. It is the constant background of our thoughts in all our approaches to God.

Since love is the test of our sincerity towards God, the examination of conscience should be made in the light of love. We should not begin by asking ourselves: What sins have I committed? but: Have I done many things or even one thing out of perfect love? This is a crippling question. It enables us to see that there is nothing quite perfect in our lives and it gives us a good yardstick to judge the whole of our day's employments.

I personally like to write down my sins. I feel that in this way the actual self-accusation in the confessional can be more than a mere feat of memory. I can give all my energy to meaning what I say. But people differ in these matters.

Older penitents may also be advised not to say their official "penance", as it is called, immediately after their confession. This "penance" is only a token satisfaction and it helps us to let some time intervene before saying it in order to give ourselves time to express in other ways a deep, contrite love of the community our sins have injured. We may want to offer God some penitential exercise like fasting, in addition. In these ways we guarantee the genuineness of our sorrow which is the soul of penance. The "penance" given us by the priest might even be left over until just before the next day's Mass when we can offer ourselves with Christ to God the Father in thanksgiving. We will immediately have the Father's loving reply: the gift of his Son, our saviour, in communion.

These are only a few of the ways in which penance can become more of a sacramental celebration. I should even venture to suggest that the whole of this day when we prepare for confession and make satisfaction for our sins is drenched in sacramental graces, strictly so called.

The question, How frequently ought we to go to confession? can only be answered in general terms. Is regular, say weekly or fortnightly reception of this sacrament beneficial? Is it a genuine expression of sorrow, a sorrow like that of a father mourning the death of his son, to borrow an image from Jeremiah? Does it make us more sensitive to our sinfulness and not less? If we can reply to these questions with a firm and completely truthful "Yes", then we shall benefit immensely from regular confession. This applies even to the confession of venial sins, particularly since the sacramental graces will make us more and more aware of our generally sinful condition, more sensitive to the holiness of God. My intention from the first was not to oppose regular confession but to lay down the conditions for making such regular confession fruitful and not a mere matter of routine.

VIII

MARRIAGE IN SCRIPTURE[1]

CHAPTER VI, on penance in scripture, made frequent reference back to what had been said on baptism, since the one is meant to be a kind of repetition of the other. And the subject was elaborated through the scriptural image of the broken marriage-bond, in which the reality of repentance comes across to us most clearly. It is that image which provides the link with this chapter on marriage. If God's relationship with us takes on most meaning in terms of marriage, the obverse is also true. Marriage is only seen in its right perspective if we express it in terms of our relationship with God.

Here, as much as anywhere else, if not more so, we need to rescripturize ourselves, to go back to the sources to re-discover for ourselves God's mind on the subject. It is true that in theory we hold marriage in the highest esteem, and can quote *Casti Connubii* backwards. But in actual fact we are the heirs of a culture which has often been almost manichaean in its attitude towards marriage. I am thinking not only of St Augustine who went on record with the remarkable statement that nothing but the bearing of children distinguishes the marriage-chamber from the brothel; that apart from this husbands are nothing else but shameful lovers, and wives nothing else but prostitutes. I am thinking of people much more recent than Augustine, great theologians like Suarez who (as Mgr Knox pointed out) in the index to his *Opera Omnia* has got only one reference

---

[1] Parts of this chapter have already appeared in *Scripture*, October, 1956, and *The Clergy Review*, May, 1959. They are reproduced and expanded here with permission.

under the word *Mulier* or Woman: "Cf. *Scandalum*." I am
thinking of writers more recent even than Suarez, stretching
right down to our own days, who think of marriage in something of the way Oscar Wilde did, as "a rather naughty sacrament", with the idea at the back of their minds that the sexual
urge in mankind is an indelicate if not disgusting business,
which ideally ought to be suppressed altogether, or sublimated
into something more ennobling, except that most of our people
could not manage that and so the Church reluctantly blesses
them. But the best people, of course, remain unmarried.

The attitude stems, one supposes, from the fact that for
centuries the Church has been run by men, and in those areas
where men have not been able to take over, by nuns; but in
either case by celibates. So that for centuries, whatever we may
say in theory, marriage has in practice been down-graded in the
Church. This has influenced all of us, as can be gauged from
the tone of voice in which we tell our children that marriage is,
of course, *also* a vocation—almost as if, without it, the supply
of celibates might run out. It is an attitude which is based on
the unchristian distinction we are always making between the
body and the soul, as if salvation was a matter for the soul alone,
and the body was only a hindrance to it. It is an attitude which
contrasts starkly with the bible, the Old Testament as well as
the New. What does the bible say on the subject of sex and
marriage? We shall look simply at three pages of it to try to
re-orientate ourselves.

Genesis

Let us begin where the bible begins, with the opening pages
of Genesis. Presumably there is no longer any need to insist
that it would be stupid to look for any kind of scientific information in these pages. It is a great pity that people ever did look
for it, and got so excited about the rib and the apple and the
figleaves—whether it was to shore them up or to pull them

down—that they left themselves no time to find out what the text was really getting at. We have mercifully progressed beyond that stage. We know now that the author was making no claim to be scientific, and that all attempts to show that he was are faintly ridiculous, like trying to confer a B.Sc. on him. He accepted, quite unselfconsciously, the ideas, the literary forms and the vocabulary of his own times as the framework and the tools with which he was going to say something infinitely more important. What he was concerned to tell his readers was not *how* or *when* the universe and mankind came to be: on that scientific question he was clearly as ignorant as the rest of us were until about a century ago. He was concerned with the infinitely more important question of *what* the world and mankind is. In other words, he was concerned not with a history or a geology or an anthropology, but with a theology, and a theology directed precisely against the kind of dualistic or manichean paganism which still infects our own thinking. A theology, then, and part of that theology is, naturally enough, a theology of marriage.

Imagine a world with a far more depressing philosophy than the one that surrounds us today, where the word "god" means a whole pantheon of grotesque powers constantly at war with each other; where the elements themselves are deified into something eternal and evil, independent of the gods and hostile to them; where the universe reaches its present shape only after an endless struggle betweeen the gods. Imagine that, and then turn to the simplicity, calm and grandeur of Genesis:

> In the beginning, *God* created the heavens and the earth, and all they contain (Gen. 1¹).

There is a majestic dignity about such an opening, where the one God of the Hebrews, supreme and eternal, is introduced with such sublime assurance that he can be presumed as an unarguable fact. It is to him that all things owe their existence, so that they appear without effort at a word from his mouth. And as the inventory is made, in all its order and beauty—light

and darkness, earth and sky, sea and dry land, trees and vegeta-
tion, fish and reptiles, wild beasts and tame—each item is
greeted with the refrain: "And God saw that it was good." All
of it of his making, and in accordance with his will. We will look
in vain among the ancient literatures of other peoples for such
a categorical expression of their faith. This is something unique.

As with the universe, so with man. Here, the world for which
Genesis was written was just as pessimistic. When your universe
has been deified into malignant powers which are constantly at
war with each other, then your man can be little more than a
cog in their machine, a pitiful creature whose only reaction to
them is fear, and a constant concern to placate them. In such a
world man's life is cheap, hard, uncertain, and at the mercy of
the gods who envy him even his happiness.

This is the sort of background against which we ought to read
Genesis, to appreciate its defence of man's dignity. And how
superbly it is done; how well it is, if you like, stage-managed,
with man deliberately kept back in the wings as the last item,
the star turn. In comparison with this, the rest of creation has
appeared almost as a divine aside: "Let there be light, let there
be a firmament, let the earth bring forth living creatures, and it
was so." But not man. No mass-production for him. He is
unique, and demands God's undivided attention: "Let *us* make
man." In fact, "Let us make him in *our own* image and likeness."
None of that for the other creatures. They were like the sea they
came out of or the earth on which they swarmed. But man is
like God. Man is a reflection of the God that has been described
in the preceding verses, someone who shares his goodness, his
capacity for order, his dominion over the rest of creation, his
creative power. The mere thought of it is so overpowering that
the author suddenly bursts into poetry:

> And God created man in his own image
> In the image of God he created him
> Male and female he created them.

You can almost hear the applause of the audience.

And when chapter 2 gives us another account of creation, it is really only to make the same point. Here man comes first in the list instead of last, but the emphasis is exactly the same—that he cannot be lumped along with the rest of creation. He is unique, and all the rest—plants, springs, trees, rivers, birds and beasts—is made for him. This time the story is much more picturesque, with God as a kind of potter modelling man with his own hands and breathing into him his own breath. But we won't be so prosaic about it that we miss the point: the unique relationship which man, of all creatures, has with God. And if that relationship is illustrated further by mention of a garden in which God walks with Adam in the cool of the evening, we won't try to find the garden on a map. Could anyone have devised a more dramatic way of expressing the intimacy with himself that God planned for man from the beginning? It is we who have concocted the fabrication of an Old Testament God of thunder and terror and fear. It is not so in Genesis.

And as with man, so obviously with woman. For the ancient world woman was little more than a superior beast of burden, one of the things a man possessed. You had an ass, some cows, a dozen sheep . . . and a woman. And when that world deified womanhood and the sexual act, woman was only degraded a step further. When man makes himself the slave of the goddess of sex, woman becomes the slave of man.

Into such an atmosphere our Genesis text comes again like a breath of fresh air. The whole of the animal world is deliberately drawn up for review, and Adam scans the whole fantastic procession simply to emphasize that it is not among them that his partner is to be found. What we are looking for is something befitting the dignity that has already been conferred on him. And it is this that God eventually produces, a help "meet" for him, someone equal in rank to him, who can be his partner and companion. If this truth is again dramatically acted out, with God now as a kind of surgeon administering the anaesthetic and performing the operation, don't let us get hot under the collar.

We could hardly have invented a more vivid symbol of the fact that, in God's design, woman really is identical in nature with man, bone of his bone and flesh of his flesh, made of the same stuff as he is, equal with him and so worthy of him.

And so, finally, marriage. If that is what man is, and that is what in God's design woman is, then you can only give a shout of joy at their marriage, as the climax of creation:

> This, at last, is a companion fit for man!
> This is why a man leaves his father and mother
> to find an even closer relationship with his wife;
> these two become one flesh (Gen. 2²⁴).

Woman has been made for man, and man is, one could say' incomplete until she finds again that place next to his heart where he misses her. If man has been made by God to be the king of creation, then marriage has been designed to be his crown.

That is already a fairly remarkable theology of marriage, one which can give even the modern reader pause for thought. But the author does not stop there. This is the ideal. This is the man-woman relationship as God planned it. But he knows as well as we do that this is not marriage as we experience it in the world as it is now. What went wrong? Why did this plan fail when, as even we would say, everything in the garden was so lovely? The answer lies in chapter 3, with the serpent, the tree, the apple and the figleaves.

How was it that we ever took this magnificent chapter so literally, and wondered whether the author was telling us which trees are good for you and which bad for you, or why serpents crawl on their belly when all decent animals have legs, and so on? After all, he has tied immense labels to both of them, to warn us that he was thinking of something rather more sinister than a bite out of an apple. This tree, he says, is the knowledge of good and evil. Its fruit, he says, will make a man like God. King David had that sort of knowledge, and so had his son Solomon. Both were celebrated by Israelite tradition as paragons of wisdom because they had the sort of penetrating mind which can distinguish, as not all of us can, between what is really good and what is really evil[1]. But they had it as a gift from God. They had it only because God allowed them to share his own wisdom. As a right, this knowledge of good and evil belongs to God alone. He alone determines what shall be called good, and what evil. He will give this knowledge to the man who humbly asks for it. But the beginning of this wisdom is reverent fear of the Lord to whom it alone belongs by right (Prov. 1[7], 9[10], 15[33], Ps. 111(110)[10]). If a man snatches at it independently of God, if he claims the right to make his own good and evil, then he is equivalently setting himself up as his own god. And we do it in every sin we commit. Equivalently we say: "I am going to call this good, whatever God calls it." There is sarcasm in the words of God which conclude the whole scene, but also bitter truth: "Behold, man has become exactly like ourselves, deciding his own good and evil."

Instead of fussing about the images and symbols which the author has used to express this truth, we should admire the accuracy with which he has put his finger on the root cause of all sin: man's decision to be his own god. This, he says, is what has destroyed God's harmonious plan, marriage included. This, he says, is the origin of the discord and tension which are to follow from chapter 4 onwards, and of which every reader will be well aware. This again is the kind of penetrating insight which can make even the modern reader stop and examine his conscience.

Does he say anything more than that? Is he leaving original sin as generic as that or does he want to suggest anything more specific? It is extraordinary how widespread is the conviction that he does suggest something more, and that original sin has something to do with sex. Now this may be because some people suspect that there is something unwholesome about sex anyway. But there are other people too, scripture scholars of all times,

---

[1] See 2 Sam. 14[7], 1 Kings 3[9-12], 4[29-34], Prov. 2[6], Wisd. 8[19]-9[12], Ecclus. 2[15].

dramatists like Milton and Shaw, who have also taken it for granted that the knowledge of good and evil was really the knowledge of what we call "the facts of life", and that the forbidden fruit was the use of the sexual faculties. It is the act of procreation, the suggestion is, which would make man most like his creator, and is therefore forbidden. It was man's snatching of this divine life-force which put him at loggerheads with God, and which is the cause of all his shame and sorrow. Is there anything in this?

We shall let St Augustine speak, to redeem himself for the extraordinary statement quoted earlier. One does not need to be a brilliant latinist to grasp the general drift of his opinion on the suggestion. *Illud*, he said, *est ridiculum*. And it is. It would contradict the whole purpose of the author, who designed chapter 2 precisely to show the wonder and beauty of marriage. It was God, he said, who made man and woman sexually different and complementary, and he presumably knew the purpose as well as we do. No, it was not the author of Genesis who thought marriage something shady. In fact it was just the other way round, as we have already seen. It was the pagans among whom the author lived who had debased marriage by regarding woman as man's slave, a toy made for his convenience and pleasure. It was precisely in view of this degraded notion of his contemporaries that the author extolled the dignity of marriage as God designed it. He was certainly not one to suggest that sin is to be identified with the marriage act; this was an essential part of God's plan for mankind.

But he could suggest that sin is to be identified with a perversion of that plan. In fact, if there is any connexion at all between chapter 3 (the serpent, the tree, the apple) and chapter 2 (the creation of man and woman), that is presumably what he did suggest. If he has given such prominence in chapter 2 to womanhood and marriage as the climax of God's design, and if the fulfilment of that design does not come until the birth of Cain in chapter 4, then presumably the sin of the intervening chapter 3 is meant to be seen as an interruption of that design. In other words, the whole make-up of chapter 2 suggests that it is precisely in this matter of marriage that man has, in chapter 3, disfigured the work of God. Perhaps the popular conviction about the meaning of the forbidden fruit is not so far out after all.

To put it more clearly, what the author of Genesis is pointing to as the root of all sin is not the use of the sexual faculties, but the deification of them, the making of them into an object of worship. This, it was stated above, is exactly what the Canaanites had done: they had made a god of sex. The god was symbolized by the serpent, and his cult consisted in the unconditional surrender of his devotees to their desires. It was this cult which had led to the degradation of woman in their society; the one went with the other. Once woman is worshipped merely for her sexual attraction, she is necessarily reduced to the level of a beast.

Now it is this cult which the author of Genesis considered to be a blow at the very heart of a God-designed universe. In the right order of things woman was neither a goddess nor a slave, but the creature of God and the companion of man. In the right order of things procreation was not a mastering of the divine life-force, but a blessing given by God to those who humbly ask for it. To snatch that power out of the hands of God and to dedicate it to one's own pleasure, that is the worship of false gods. If sin consists ultimately and always in man's attempt to claim independence of God, this sin is, for the author, its vilest example.

That does not mean that man's first disobedience consisted in fact in such a degradation of his marriage. The author of Genesis has no information about the precise nature of the first sin. If he has described it in these terms and painted it in these colours, it is because, for his particular readers, that was the most striking example of man making his own good and evil. We have only to glance through the prophets to see what a fascination this fertility cult always held for the Jews, from one end of their history to the other. There is hardly a page on which Isaiah and Jeremiah and the rest do not plead with their people to leave these false gods and return to the Lord. For such readers, and in such an atmosphere, this worship of sex represented the power of evil at its most devilish. Nor can we pretend that this particular emphasis has lost any of its relevance for our age. At 3,000 years' distance the atmosphere seems strangely to linger on, murky as ever. The Canaanites were not the last to set up a sex-symbol and worship it. The original readers of Genesis were not the last to feel the attraction of it pulling at their heartstrings, or to need the promise of one who would crush the head of this man-made god.

There, then, is the teaching of the author of Genesis on marriage, as a deliberate counter-blast to the paganism of his time, and of ours too. As we can see, he is no starry-eyed romantic. He has no delusions about the dangers that surround marriage, or the perversity with which man constantly sabotages it. But he is no manichean pessimist either, as if sex were something too hot to handle and marriage a sort of *faute de mieux*. He is willing to recognize what a shambles men are always making of it—the disorder they are always making of God's order, the shame they are always introducing into the innocence he planned, the bitterness and loneliness they are always bringing into the intimate and loving union he meant it to be. But his thesis is a positive one: it is a theme of the love and order and beauty that marriage is and can be, because God made it so.

An exact echo of this attitude may be found in the rest of the Old Testament. On the one hand, there is no lack of realism in the marriages described there. Its pages are filled with stories of divorce, polygamy, concubinage, squabbling wives, adultery and lust. There is no dearth of marriages which follow the pattern of Adam and Eve's in unhappiness, failure and disappointment. The very language it uses is a confession of that reality. The word for a husband is "lord", someone who lords it over his wife; the word for marriage is "to acquire property", so that the wife was often seen as a piece of household furniture, just as she was among the pagans: "Thou shalt not covet thy neighbour's ox or ass or sheep or slave or wife"—it was all one. But on the other hand there is no dearth of stories about marriages which are not a caricature of God's plan. We have only to think of Tobit and Sarah, of Elkanah and Hannah, of Isaac and Rebekah, or of Jacob and the Rachel whom he loved so much that the seven years he worked to win her seemed like so many days (words which Mgr Knox suggested should be written up in letters of gold over every seminary and novitiate door). Where else would one find such a loving description of the perfect housewife as the one which forms the lesson for feasts of Holy Women (Prov. 31$^{10-31}$), or as can be read in the companion book of Ecclesiasticus:

> Happy is the husband of a good wife;
> the number of his days will be doubled.
> A loyal wife rejoices her husband,
> and he will complete his days in peace.
> A good wife is a great blessing;
> she will be granted among the blessings of the man who fears the Lord.
> Whether rich or poor, his heart is glad,
> and at all times his face is cheerful. . . .
> A wife's charm delights her husband,
> and her skill puts fat on his bones.
> A silent wife is a gift of the Lord,
> and there is nothing so precious as a disciplined soul.
> A modest wife adds charm to charm,
> and no balance can weigh the value of a chaste soul.
> Like the sun rising in the heights of the Lord,
> so is the beauty of a good wife in her well-ordered home.
> Like the shining lamp on the holy lampstand,
> so is a beautiful face on a stately figure (Ecclus. 26$^{1-4, 13-17}$).

What a background of true and happy marriage that supposes.

The prophets

For our second page of scripture, we shall look very briefly at the prophets. We have already seen how it was the prophets who first used this reality of marriage to illustrate the relationship of Israel to God, and who first spoke of God not only as the creator, king and father but also as the husband of Israel, and of Israel not only as the creature, subject and son but also as the bride of God. It is the perfect image to convey the fact that the relationship into which God has entered with us is not a distant one that remains on a purely juridical level, but a personal one, a relationship of intimacy and closeness such as we would not have dared imagine possible. The image is used by the prophets precisely because it contains within it that two-fold aspect already revealed by Genesis, of something designed perfect by God, and yet constantly thrown out of gear by man's perversity.

Hosea used the image because he had firsthand evidence of that double reality in his own marriage. But he was not the last to use it. From his time onwards it became a commonplace in prophetical literature, to give rise to such lyrical passages as the following:

> Go and proclaim in the hearing of Jerusalem, Thus says the Lord:
> I remember the devotion of your youth,
> your love as a bride,
> how you followed me in the wilderness. . . .
> But long ago you broke your yoke and burst your bonds,
> and you said, I will not serve.
> Yes, upon every high hill and under every green tree
> you bowed down as a harlot. . . .
> Though you wash yourself with lye and use much soap,
> the stain of your guilt is still before me. . . .
> How can you say, I am not defiled,
> I have not gone after the Baals?
> Look at your way in the valley;
> know what you have done—
> a restive young camel interlacing her tracks,

a wild ass used to the wilderness,
in her heat sniffing the wind!
Who can restrain her lust?
None who seek her need weary themselves;
in her month they will find her!
Watch out! your feet will go unshod
and your throat thirsty!
But you said, It is hopeless for I have loved strangers,
and after them I will go. . . .
If a man divorces his wife
and she goes from him and becomes another man's wife,
will he return to her? (Jer. 2²–3¹).

Thus says the Lord God to Jerusalem: Your origin and your birth are of the land of the Canaanites; your father was an Amorite, and your mother a Hittite. And as for your birth, on the day you were born your navel string was not cut, nor were you washed with water to cleanse you, nor rubbed with salt, nor swathed with bands. No eye pitied you, to do any of these things to you out of pity for you; but you were cast out on the open field, for you were abhorred, on the day that you were born.

And when I passed by you, and saw you weltering in your blood, I said to you in your blood, Live, and grow up like a plant of the field. And you grew up and became tall and arrived at full maidenhood. . . .

When I passed by you again and looked upon you, behold, you were at the age for love; and I spread my skirt over you, and covered your nakedness: yea, I plighted my troth to you and entered into a covenant with you, says the Lord God, and you became mine. . . . And your renown went forth among the nations because of your beauty, for it was perfect through the splendour which I had bestowed upon you, says the Lord God (Ezek. 16³⁻¹⁴).

You will forget the shame of your youth,
and the reproach of your widowhood you will remember no more.
For your Maker is your husband, the Lord of hosts is his name. . . .
For the Lord has called you like a wife forsaken and grieved,
like a wife of youth when she is cast off, says your God.
For a brief moment I forsook you,
but with great compassion I will gather you.
In overflowing wrath for a moment I hid my face from you,
but with everlasting love I will have compassion on you,
says the Lord your Redeemer (Isaiah 54⁴⁻⁸).   ˙

The figure in fact became such a commonplace that it was possible for the Deuteronomic writer to tell the whole history of Israel (Deuteronomy–Joshua–Judges–Samuel–Kings) with this as the underlying theme, so that the story of Israel could be seen for what it was, the love-story of God, the generous and zealous lover who will not go back on his word to his bride, and who loves her even when he has to chastize her. And, of course, that is basically also the theme of the Song of Solomon, which uses the marriage imagery with an openness and explicit frankness which have made some of its readers raise their eyebrows. It is true that some commentators try to cover their embarrassment by desperately appealing to the lilies throughout the poem as symbols of virginity, and support their interpretation by stressing how frequently the woman in the song is referred to as "sister". But this is precisely the language that was used in contemporary Egyptian love-poetry. Nor does it need much imagination to realize that there is no brother-sister relationship in such a passage as:

> How fair and pleasant you are,
> O loved one, delectable maiden!
> You are stately as a palm tree,
> and your breasts are like its clusters.
> I say I will climb this palm tree
> and lay hold of its branches.
> Oh, may your breasts be like clusters of the vine,
> and the scent of your breath like apples,
> and your kisses like the best wine
> that goes down smoothly,
> gliding over lips and teeth (Song 7[6-9]).

No. This is the realistic language which the author decided to use to express the intimacy of God's relationship with Israel. It is a language which will influence profoundly the page of scripture which we are going to look at next. But this also needs to be said: if this reveals to us something of the passion and tenderness of God's love, what should it reveal to us of the sacredness in all human love? If God has chosen these physical terms to express his relationship with us, what right have we to treat the physical side of marriage as something indelicate or merely animal, something which is only redeemed by having as many children as possible? It is not the fruitfulness of marriage that God has, as it were, canonized by taking it up to refer it to himself. On the contrary, it is a question here of the personal love-relationship, the "love unadorned", the insatiable yearning of husband and wife for each other, whether that love is still on its honeymoon as in the Song, or has been disappointed, in spite of children, as in Hosea. That is the aspect of marriage which God has seen fit to turn to his purpose. This does not mean that sex is not dangerous. Everything sacred is dangerous; that is what the word sacred means. But when God has been so rhapsodic about its wonder and beauty, should we not at least try to share his wonder?

St Paul

For the last page of scripture to help us review our ideas about marriage, we will turn to St Paul, who is still so widely and so strangely regarded as a woman-hater. Let us content ourselves with one paragraph of his, the remarkable one in Ephesians which picks up the marriage imagery used so freely by the prophets.

Paul wrote the epistle to the Ephesians in the year 62, towards the end of his life. It is the calmest of all his writings, with none of the anxiety about heresy which marks all his other letters. He is content here to put forward, quite positively, a synthesis of the Christian mystery as it has by now matured in his mind, convinced that this will satisfy all the searchings of the Mediterranean world for a philosophy of life. The sum content of this mystery is Christ, a Christ who possesses from eternity all the fullness of Godhead, and in whose becoming man therefore the longed-for union between man and God has been finally achieved. This union between God and man is extended through all time in the Church, which is the body of Christ, filled at every moment with his fulness. We can only think of Christ and the Church as distinct from each other, as husband and wife are: they are really one flesh, one body. In the Church we are "in Christ"—the phrase occurs again and again in the epistle—and, moreover, in Christ we are where Christ is, which is where God is, in heaven.

For Paul, this sublime synthesis of Christianity is not simply something for the theologian's speculation. This is the guiding principle which must govern the attitude of each one of us to such everyday matters as honesty and patience and humility and purity. This is the reality which must form the background to the everyday relationship between a slave and his master, between a child and its parents . . . and between a wife and her husband:

> Wives, be subject to your husbands, as to the Lord. For the husband is the head of the wife as Christ is the head of the Church, his body. . . . As the Church is subject to Christ, so let wives also be subject in everything to their husbands. Husbands, love your wives, as Christ loved the Church and gave himself up for her, that he might sanctify her. . . . Even so husbands should love their wives as their own bodies . . . (which they) nourish and cherish, as Christ does the Church, because we are members of his body. "For this reason a man shall leave his father and mother and be joined to his wife, and the two shall become one." This is a great mystery, and I take it to mean Christ and the Church (Eph. 5$^{22-32}$).

What is Paul doing here? We must watch him very closely or we shall miss the point. He is doing the very opposite of what we might have expected him to do. He has quoted both of the pages in which we have been searching for guidance, Genesis and the prophets with their marriage-metaphor. We therefore expect him to use that marriage relationship, as the prophets had done, to throw light on the God-man relationship. Instead he has done the very opposite. He has used the God-man relationship to throw light on marriage.

In doing this, in turning the Old Testament metaphor inside out, he has done what the New Testament does repeatedly. Over and over again the New Testament takes up a term which we think we understand, and then turns it back to front to tell us we have got it the wrong way round. The Old Testament had called God a Father. We think of this as a metaphor. We know what human fathers are like, how they love, protect, support and educate their children; God must be something like that. And the New Testament says no. Human fatherhood is the metaphor, a faint copy of the original. The only real Father is God, and it is after him that every other fatherhood is named (Eph. 3¹⁵). So it is when we refer to Christ as the bread of life and think that he must be something like the bread we know, which nourishes, sustains and strengthens us. But Christ calls himself the true bread (John 6³²). It is our bread which is the metaphor, the imitation which tries to do for us on an infinitely lower level what Christ does as our real food. So it is also when we call Christ the vine and think that our relationship to him must be something like that of a branch which depends for its life on the vinestock, and which can only die if it is cut off. And again we are wrong. Christ is the true vine (John 15¹), the original one. Any other tree we know is only a copy, and we won't really understand the working of it until we have grasped something of the mystery of our utter dependence on the lifegiving tree which is Christ.

Now it is the kind of thing that St Paul is saying about marriage. We thought, and indeed the prophets taught us to think, that human marriage was a way in which we could speak, metaphorically, of God's union with men. St Paul is telling us that it is really the other way round. It is human marriage which is the metaphor. The true reality, the exemplar of which every human marriage is only an imperfect copy, is the union between God and men. And that original model, that unique love of God which would draw all mankind into his embrace, of which every other union of two in one flesh from Adam and Eve downwards has been only a faint copy, is finally revealed to us in all its fullness when we see the body of Christ, where God and man have become one flesh, a body which continues for all time as the Church. In the Church the marriage between God and creation is consummated.

That is the prototype. That always was the prototype, even before Adam and Eve. That always was the plan by which God intended to bring the world back to himself. St Paul calls it *the* mystery—the word occurs throughout the epistle—the great secret, the hidden plan which was slowly unfolded in the history of Israel and which is revealed now in its fulness. And if all the marriages that ever took place were a kind of reflection of that plan, if every human couple were a kind of unconscious echo of this original couple in the mind of God—Christ and the Church which is his body—what shall we say of Christian marriage and the Christian couple?

A paraphrase of the passage may help to drive the point home:

> The wife should surrender to her husband as if to Christ, since he is her head, just as Christ is the head and saviour of his body, the Church. . . . Just as the Church surrenders to Christ, so should the wife surrender in all things to her husband.
>
> The husband on his side, as a counterpart to that surrender, to evoke that surrender, should (not dominate his wife or lord it over her, but) love his wife in the way that Christ loved the Church. It was for the Church that he gave himself up in order to bring it to God. . . . It is in this way that the husband should love his wife, as if she were his own body . . . which he takes such care to keep fed and free from harm. For this is precisely how Christ loves us, the limbs that make up his body, the Church. Genesis spoke of a man leaving his father and mother in order to be united to his wife in one flesh. Those words contain a great mystery, the mystery which has finally been revealed in the union between Christ and his Church.

There in short is Paul's contribution to the theology of marriage. He has transfigured it into something even more breath-taking than Genesis and the prophets made of it. Marriage always was something sacred, they had assured us. But now it has been shown to us as a replica of God's marriage with mankind in Christ, a living witness to the world of his indescribable love. And it is that by its very nature, quite irrespective of how many children that love produces. Quite apart from that consideration, the love with which man and wife give themselves utterly to each other is a mirror in which men may see the relationship between Christ and the Church. To grow in that love is not something which conflicts with their spiritual life. It *is* their spiritual life.

But it is even more than a mirror; it re-creates that relationship and makes it real over and over again. And what it makes real above all is the paschal mystery. Because God became one flesh with us not only in the incarnation; that was only the first step. The purpose of the incarnation was not achieved until that one flesh had been glorified in Christ's death and resurrection. It was in that that God's marriage with mankind was completed, when the life which God had to give filled the body of Christ which we call the Church, and Christ said: "It is consummated." It is this that Christian marriage re-enacts, as all the sacraments do. Christian marriage, just like Christian baptism and Christian penance and the Christian Eucharist, is the living out of the paschal mystery of our lives. That is why, just like those other sacraments, it involves the cross. We cannot avoid that here, any more than in any other aspect of the Christian life, or it would not be the Christian life. But it is the paschal cross, illuminated with the light of Easter day.

IX

MARRIAGE IN THE WORLD TODAY

A COLLEAGUE ONCE SAID to me that the areas of human life actually ruled by intelligence are remarkably few. Man is defined as "rational animal", and it is thought that it is the rational in him that distinguishes man. So it is. Yet the animal, the instinctual in us, the intense desire we have to follow the well-tried and familiar patterns of previous behaviour—to the despite of a more reasonable and more enlightened way—these are strong in us. Hence the painful character of any *aggiornamento* whether it be in a club, in society at large, or in the Church.

But the arduousness of using reason is evidenced not only in adapting to new experiences but in an enlightened—as opposed to a prejudiced—attitude to things that are old.

If only we would *look* more intensely at the things we take for granted as valid and valuable, our lives would be all the richer. This is especially true of fontal things, things which when deeply appreciated alter the whole strategy of our thinking or our behaviour.

A genius has been defined as someone with an infinite capacity for taking pains. This sounds like a definition concocted by a harried and persevering civil servant who has felt within him an inspiration to greatness. I don't know of any simple and conclusive characterization of genius but certainly one form of it is the ability to question the obvious or, perhaps, to ask questions of the obvious. By testing and probing the elementary and basic features of our thinking we lay the foundations for future building and, on occasions, make startling discoveries.

Let me give one or two examples of what I mean by "emphasizing the elementary".

If we are teachers, the most important of our achievements is when we get our students to think for themselves. The teacher succeeds when he gets the pupils to see that he, as an individual, is dispensable; when the subject has become more important than he is; and when the students have grasped the know-how of *research* into the subject itself.

An example similar to this refers not to a habit of study but to a quality of mind, namely, tolerance. A man who has, by slow, painful measures, rooted out prejudice and intolerance from his soul, who is able to recognize and correct any dogmatic bias as soon as it appears and sticks like a leech to the evidence —such a one has effected a fundamental and lasting change in his character.

The last example I will give is of a philosophic nature. Since everything if it is to be known must, as we say, "come into the mind", the philosopher who can say most exactly what mind is and what knowing is is clearly nearest to solving all the problems which have agitated all the philosophers throughout the ages.

If a student has but once the experience of thinking for himself; if a man but once casts aside the shackles of intolerance to breathe the air of freedom; if a philosopher has a previously unattained insight into what knowing is, there is a radical or fontal change wrought in each of them.

The same is true, I suggest, of anyone who sees and ponders deeply the role of the family in society. The effects will be noticeable on the whole range of his personal and social communing with others.

In this chapter, I am not going to try to be original in any sense, but simply to try to think through a little more persistently than usual and with the help of social and psychological research something that all of us have always taken for granted. We shall simply be doing that which is rarely done but which is exhilarating nonetheless—researching into the obvious. My aim can be crystallized in this question: What is the role of the family in society?

Changing forms of society

Firstly, what is society? A simple answer would be a mutually recognized system of relationships. There is no society between trees and stones, as there is, for instance, between animals. The higher the capacity to make relationships the higher is the capacity to enter into society. With man there is not a mere spatio-temporal relationship as with physical objects, nor only the sensible relationships of animals. Man, as we said in the first chapter, is spiritual: he can make spiritual relationships with God and with his fellows. The depth of his converse with himself, his knowledge of himself is matched and complemented by the depth and breadth of his outward relationships. Man being spiritual, in general, abhors the purely animal. As one author puts it: "Human desires are not simply the biological impulses of hunger for eating and of sex for mating. Indeed, man is an animal for whom mere animality is indecent."[1] Man needs to dignify eating by table manners, civilized taboos we may call them. He needs to sanctify sex by courtship and marriage.

An elementary study of anthropology shows that the forms which society takes, the actual social embodiment of man's spirit, vary according to time and locality. The same is true of the "family". The family is a grouping of blood-relatives—the community being, in the words of Aristotle, a union of families. But the size and structure of the family alters over the ages.

It is only comparatively recently that young married couples

---

[1] Bernard Lonergan, *Insight, A study in human understanding,* London, 1957, p. 187.

began to found a family *of their own*. Founding a family on two people probably hadn't been tried since the days of Adam and Eve. In fact, it is the nature and smallness of present-day family-grouping that accounts for so many of the strains and so much of the inexperience to be found in today's marriages. Before our times, a family meant two, three, perhaps four generations living in close proximity, assisting each other in the daily chores and giving each other psychological support. Such a system, as recent research shows, continues to a limited extent, in certain areas of London's East End like Bethnal Green. Not, it is true, to the extent of three generations living in the same small city house, which would indeed be intolerable, but to the extent that succeeding generations live within walking distance of each other, so that throughout life a mother can be her daughter's best friend, helping and advising her and comforting her in all the stresses of married life.

The break-up of the patriarchal state of society has loosened family bonds. Women can easily get extra-familial employment. Hitherto, as one book puts it rather bluntly, "For the woman particularly there was little refuge outside the family except the nunnery or prostitution."[1]

Women have as a consequence gained in freedom and have lost in stability. This, it seems, is inevitable and not to be deplored: the realizing of it helps us to fortify the factors that make for stability in a changing world. For example, it is surely a source of sadness that so many dwellings are being pulled down in our cities to make way for offices which are then un-tenanted for several years. Those original dwellings, by govern-mental action, should have been replaced by other dwellings so that young married couples should not have to move miles away from their kith and kin to find a place to live. They are, in the process, uprooted from the community in which they are brought up and into which they fit, and made to live—the woman particularly—in a kind of isolation on a new but often

[1] R. M. Maciver and C. H. Page, *Society*, London, 1962, p. 267.

soul-less building estate far from the places and the people they have known and loved.

It is not only the family structure which changes in differing cultures but also family functions. Miss Margaret Mead, for example, tells us that in the Manus tribe the father takes the principal role in family life. He it is who plays the part of "the tender solicitous indulgent guardian, while the mother takes second place in the child's affection".[1] This is a reversal of family functions as we know them.

It is clear, then, that we are discussing the role of the family in *our* society. Studies in comparative anthropology will forewarn us against absolutizing what are, in effect, contingent and passing products of our own society.

The advantages of monogamous marriage

The first major question we shall ask is: What are the advantages to the partners of monogamous marriage? Apart from the obvious things, I mean, like sexual satisfaction, companionship, stability of home-life and so on.

Some psychologists express it like this. We have a need to be loved and to love.

A need to be loved. This primal need is first met by our parents, especially our mother. It was a forgiving love: we were forgiven and accepted sometimes when we least deserved it. This is the human analogue of God's forgiving grace. Think of the difference between a child brought up in this way with the continual experience of being forgiven, and an institution-child whose delicts are impersonal and sometimes automatically punishable and who has not known the sweetness of loving forgiveness. We need to be loved. "One of the unconscious satisfactions sought in marriage is a continuous, secure form of love which can replace that of our parents. Even parental love had its imperfections." It had to be shared with other members

[1] *Growing up in New Guinea*, Penguin Books, London, 1963, p. 14.

of the family. "However, in married love to some extent one does have one's loved object to oneself and thus the childhood wish is met at last."[1]

Secondly, there is the need to love. "In loving we feel that the good within us is preponderant over the bad, and that we have love inside us sufficient to fulfil the needs of a partner as well as our own. Marriage is a great reassurance regarding the good within us; it is proof of our inner store of love. Sexual relations in marriage are an added reassurance."[2] A happy marital sexual relationship shows to each partner that sexual desire is a good thing, able to fulfil and satisfy the other, and especially creative and worthy when it issues in children. Since, as was mentioned in the previous chapter, there are still to be found isolated pockets of Manicheism among Christians, it is worth adding these reflections: Christ's sacrifice on the cross was his consummation of his marriage to the Church, his sanctification of the Church. Likewise every act of marriage among human beings is an act of self-sacrifice, of self-oblation, of sanctification. Every act, for Christians, is like a fresh baptism of the other, a clothing of the other with Christ. This is, I believe, good Pauline theology. We are still inclined to identify the good and ethical with the difficult, and to consider that the pleasurable cannot be holy. St Thomas Aquinas says that it is not the difficulty in loving which is important but the loving. When love is perfect there is no difficulty in loving. The easy and the pleasurable *can* be good.

The need for loving and being loved, it seems to me, is the best foundation on which to build an argument—in so far as any argument will stand—for the indissolubility of marriage as such, as opposed to that of particular marriages. For many marriages are childless but no marriage can afford to be loveless. If children alone constituted a reason for marriage's indissolu-

---

[1] W. L. Herbert and F. Jarvis, *A Modern Approach to Marriage Counselling*, London, 1959, p. 38.
[2] *Ibid.*, p. 39.

bility then many marriages should be dissoluble. But if—apart from any insight given by revelation—the reason is the mutual love which may or may not issue in children, the permanence of marriage is set upon the enduring need of the *partners* who constituted the marriage in the first place by the exchange of their loving consent. The Church's claim that all childless and post-childbearing marriages are permanent of their nature is a declaration that without such permanence the quality needed and demanded by the partners to the marriage could not be secured.

The stable and loving union between husband and wife is the only happy context for childbearing and child-upbringing. This is especially true in our day when each couple founds a family of its own.

Unfortunately, there is a kind of vicious circle to be noticed in family relationships. A person who is badly reared becomes in his turn so maladjusted as an adult that he becomes a bad husband (or wife) and a bad parent. I am not using the word "bad" in an ethical sense; perhaps it would be better to speak of unsatisfactory parents.

A child's early years

Let us begin at the beginning. When a sea-horse emerges at birth—one of a large progeny—it immediately fends for itself. It has a mother, but it has no need of mothering, hence it is not liable either to suffer the calamity of "s-mothering". A human infant does need mothering—like many other animals. But what happens to the child in his early years? Strangely enough an answer to this fontal question has only been attempted with the aid of a thorough empirical investigation in recent years.

What do researches tell us, then, of a child in the darkness and turmoil of his first unconscious years? How does he fare? Evidently he is a dependent being, but he cannot think or reason or understand; so that there is a tendency on the part of some to refuse credence to the statement that he can be made or marred for life before he begins to speak. Even theorists used to consider that the child who cannot think articulately or talk, cannot suffer decisive, long-term injury. But the inability to think or talk is probably the reason why he suffers most. He suffers in darkness. He cannot express or comprehend his fears, emotions, anxieties. Even a disturbed adolescent is in a dangerous position when he is unable to verbalize his anxieties, since the only alternative to talking them out is acting them out, with consequences always disastrous to himself and often to others.

Let us take a parallel from biological development. We know, for example, that if a mother in the sixth to the tenth week of pregnancy contracts German measles there is a serious danger that the virus will damage the unborn baby. The virus is liable to attack the eyes and the ears just then beginning to be formed, thus causing blindness or deafness or both. Those weeks are vital because then is the special period when the organs are being formed. Damage done at this time is permanent damage.

As in biological, so in emotional development. Harm, when it is done at crucial times, is liable to have vital and enduring effects. This is true even of brute animals, like monkeys, on whom numerous and ingenious experiments have been carried out.

As Bowlby in his outstanding piece of research *Maternal Care and Mental Health*[1] has pointed out, in the last thirty-five years or so we have seen "the steady growth of evidence that the quality of the parental care which a child receives in his earliest years is of vital importance for his future mental health".[2]

The child needs the experience of "a warm, intimate and continuous relationship with his mother"—or mother-substitute, a relationship in which both experience satisfaction and enjoyment. Without it we are forced to speak of maternal deprivation. Deprivation may be partial when the mother cannot

---

[1] World Health Organization, Geneva, 1952. A summarized version of this is *Child Care and the Growth of Love*, Penguin Books, 1953. References will be made to this shorter edition.

[2] Op. cit., p. 11.

give her child the loving care he needs or when he is farmed out to someone, who, though kind and loving, is a stranger. Deprivation may be complete when in institutions, residential nurseries and hospitals "the child often has no *one* person who cares for him in a personal way and with whom he may feel secure".[1]

Children have been studied in many ways, by direct observation, by looking into the histories of those who in later years are known to be mentally ill, and by follow-up studies of those who have been deprived in their early years. They have been studied, too, in many countries. All the findings support each other in a remarkable way.

Complete deprivation of maternal love of all children under about seven brings almost certain injury. "Some of the effects are clearly discernible within the first few weeks of life."[2] From the age of 6–12 months a three months bout of deprivation entails a "qualitative change, after which recovery is rarely if ever complete".[3] A provocative and sombre statement.

Even partial deprivation sets its mark on a child. It makes him an anxious individual, one who experiences an excessive need for love, powerful feelings of revenge, and arising from these last, guilt and depression. Inevitably there are nervous disorders and instability of character.

We must content ourselves with these summary remarks. In the earliest years, the child is most in need of emotional attachment to his mother. The sudden loss of it for a short time or a long time has its effect, sometimes permanently. The child after that may be afraid to enter into any future relationships, afraid of being hurt and of having to go through a similar traumatic experience again.

The central feature of all disturbances is the inability to make relationships, inadequacy for society or unsociability. The inability to accept love when it is offered is also very marked. The mother not only introduces the child to the world, gives him

[1] p. 12.   [2] p. 19.   [3] p. 24.

that security he needs, that continuous relationship which enables him to think in stable conceptual categories, she it is who enables him to accept love. She is trustworthy and so worthy of love. He has hurt her and in his child's way he has hated as well as loved her. But she has taken it all and loved him nonetheless.

The child without this experience grows into a man afraid to love for fear of being hurt and also, it may be, for fear of hurting the person he really wants to love.

Let us reflect for a moment on this tendency of unloved people to withdraw into a world of their own. To let themselves be loved is too hard, too humiliating a thing. They may be charitable, they may give in so far as they can but they cannot receive and are too proud and too afraid to let themselves be loved. They will love God but will not let God love them. They don't trust God and cannot look on him as merciful. Hence the coldness and austerity of their lives.

There is a close connection between loving and being loved. The person who genuinely loves is the lovable person, someone who is receptive of, porous to all the love that is in the air around him. He attracts love to himself. To want to be loved is not selfishness: it is the very condition of normality and of being able to love. It is the willingness to accept the burden as well as the joy of someone else's love. Karl Marx expressed it like this: "You may exchange money for goods, food, even loyalty. But man as man can only exchange love for love, confidence for confidence: 'If you love without calling forth love, that is, if your love as such does not produce love, if by means of *an expression of life* as a loving person you do not make of yourself a *loved person*, then your love is impotent, a misfortune.' "[1] Your love has failed.

Even in the emotionally deprived, the craving for love remains: though it is repressed, it always finds an outlet in a social behaviour. It may be sexual promiscuity, sadism, or theft—

[1] Quoted in E. Fromm, *The Sane Society*, London, 1963, p. 132.

especially theft. As one psychiatrist put it: "Some people when they get upset get bellyache, some get drunk, some people steal in a crazy way."[1] Theft is most commonly associated with emotional deprivation: people steal—and this is particularly true of small children—not because they are needy but because they feel unloved. Their aggressiveness is an attempt to counter and rid themselves of the strong strain of sadness which runs through their lives.

The mother, then, is irreplaceable in the formation of a normal human being. She is equipped for this role by nature, both biologically and emotionally. She communicates friendliness and security and playfulness even in the way she holds and feeds and dresses and enjoys the company of her baby. She mediates the world for him.

The father in the family

Studies of illegitimate children help by way of contrast to show the role of the father in family life. But first it should be noticed that many illegitimate children are the result not of sexual desire and biological accident but of illness. The child is often the symptom of the mother's or father's neurosis. The mother may need the child either as a love-object, or to shame dominating parents—perhaps to wound herself because she feels guilty. Human beings find it so easy to accept the guilt which is not of their deserving, and so hard to rid themselves of it. Whenever men feel pain, spontaneously, whether consciously or unconsciously, if there is no obvious scapegoat they feel guilty. The study of comparative religion yields abundant evidence of the identification of suffering and guilt. So does the life of every individual. The extreme form of self-depreciation and self-punishment is suicide. It occurs at the highest point of felt rejection by others, at the moment when the person in question feels too guilty and too unworthy to live on.

[1] D. Miller, *Growth to Freedom*, London, 1964, p. 146.

The father is needed to give emotional support to the mother. If the mother does not receive support, she communicates unconsciously her anxieties to her child. The father is also considered to bring into the home the authority which is the necessary complement of love, and so, paradoxically, giving the child a hate-object which he requires at times, and which he need not identify with his mother. The father stands, too, for the wider world of human relationships and human activities. He is like a traveller from a distant land, though he work no further from home than Fulham is from Shepherd's Bush.

I should say that what the father brings into the home as well is a gradually manifested and yet tolerated imperfection. To explain what I mean I will quote an example from D. W. Winnicott's, *The Child, The Family and The Outside World*. It concerns a girl whose father died before she was born:

> The tragedy here was that she had only an idealized father on whom to base her view of man. She had not the experience of being let down gently by a real father. In her life she easily imagined men to be ideal, which at first had the effect of bringing out the best in them. But sooner or later, inevitably, each man she got to know showed imperfections, and each time this happened she was thrown into a state of despair, and was continually complaining. As you can imagine this pattern ruined her life. How much happier she would have been if her father had been alive during her childhood, to be felt by her to be ideal, but also to be found by her to have shortcomings, and to have survived her hate of him when he disappointed her.[1]

Not only women but men as well are capable of this idealizing of the absent. Before the age of psychology Thomas Hardy in *Tess of the d'Urbervilles* characterized Tess's husband, Angel Clare, in this way: "Clare's love was doubtless ethereal to a fault, imaginative to impracticability. With these natures, corporeal presence is something less appealing than corporeal absence; the latter creating an ideal presence that conveniently drops the defects of the real."

We may still not have brought out clearly enough the *positive*

[1] Penguin Books, London, 1964, p. 117.

role of the father in child-upbringing. Miss Mead's researches into the Manus tribe show the influence that a father can have in the child's formation. C. G. Jung has also indicated the feminine characteristics that complete the psyche of the male, characteristics which are displayed in a father's tenderness and sympathy toward's his children. It is interesting to record that Mary Morse in her book *The Unattached* to which reference will be made later suggests there may be a connection between delinquency in adolescents and the break-down of *father*-child relations.

Since the mother may be stricter and sterner stuff than the father, and since we must not look for any hard and fast roles of mother and father in parent-child relations, perhaps we can safely lay down the following principle: the way husband and wife relate to their children will depend on the way they complete each other as persons.

It has truly been said that "one of the principal purposes of the family is the preservation of the art of parenthood".[1] When parents fail, society inevitably suffers.

"Where anything is growing," wrote Horace Mann, "one former is worth a thousand re-formers." The flaws found in a child's psyche—and psychic scars are as real as physical ones— are seen in enlarged form in the adult later on. Emotional deprivation is as cruel in its effects as the lack of Vitamin D which results in a child's rickety legs.

Reflections on the findings of child psychology

Certain things would seem to follow from the psychological data we have summarily brought forward.

To begin with, human beings cannot be looked at as isloated atoms. They exist in and through social relationships of which the family is the most basic. All our other attachments and affections are extensions of those we have fashioned within the

[1] Quoted in Bowlby, op. cit., pp. 77–8.

family cell. Most of our later life is spent building on the secure foundations laid in the home or struggling with the mental and emotional problems there engendered.

The National Association of Youth Clubs recently supported the pioneer work of helping the unattached—teenagers who do not belong to anyone or anything. The team of investigators found that "while the social and economic background of the unattached varied considerably, a breakdown in family relationships was a common factor in all cases. Happy parent-child relationships were the exception rather than the rule."[1] Later: "It is perhaps sufficient to say that the findings of this project add yet another piece of evidence of the overwhelming importance of a happy and stable family life."[2]

We cannot ponder too deeply that man's very nature is social. When I was a student I received the impression that man is a very wonderful being, capable of reflecting on himself, spiritual, immortal and so on. In addition he was social. This latter fact was used as an argument for weekly Mass-going. It is now evident to me that man only finds himself, comes to a sense of his own individuality in and through his union with others. The individual depends for his individuality on the community. It is only the really good "community man" who is satisfactory as an individual. The individualist, on the contrary, is one who has not come to terms with himself as an individual and is wrongly trying to find himself by a more or less complete secession from the community.

The data we have brought forward indicates also that if a child is to be cured of his emotional disturbances the family must be cured first. It is the very basic principle of social psychology that it is easier to change a group—especially a small group— than it is to change directly the individuals who compose the group. This is manifest if the individual we are dealing with is a child or a youngster. It follows that much more of our welfare

---

[1] Mary Morse, *The Unattached*, Penguin Books, London, 1964, p. 212.
[2] *Ibid.*

work should be family welfare work. In *Social Casework in Great Britain* we read: "A children's service was set up in 1948, excellent in many ways in scope and design. But the intimate relation between parents and their children, even their neglected children, seems to have been overlooked until the first few years brought home the difficulty of offering a service to children without having to deal also with parental reactions."[1] We must treat the family as a unit.

"Ultimately all case-work is family case-work."[2] The pastoral clergy above all need to keep this principle in mind because they are building on sand if they expect the child to be reliable when his family circumstances are deplorable and are likely to remain so. Teachers and youth leaders, too, have to realize how essential it is to know the home background of their charges and to have regular contact with parents. This realization is growing in fact.

If the researches of men like Bowlby are correct, the old adage that "there is no place like home" must be taken with the utmost seriousness. In the nineteenth century, when fever or cholera repeatedly swept the land, the social workers were primarily concerned with improving hygiene, insisting on drains and sewers. Today these things are "mainly the concern of the sanitary engineer".[3] Moreover, as a United Nations Congress Report on the Prevention of Crime, 1960, made plain, delinquency which is the product of bad homes actually increases in countries where, far from there being drainage and sewage problems, there are excellent housing conditions, health, medical and welfare services. A home is primarily to be thought of as "bad" not in terms of physical circumstances but in terms of human relationships. But even a home "bad" in this latter sense is better than no home at all. The chances are that a bad home is better than the best institution. Social workers are foolish to think that there is anything they can do which will remotely rival the continual care of the mother for her child or

[1] London, 1961, p. 34.   [2] *Ibid.*, p. 177.   [3] *Ibid.*, p. 22.

even her mere continual presence to him. As Clare Britton writes: "It is a problem to have to face the world without the backing of your own home and to have to explain to the world and, more important, to yourself why you have lost it."[1]

Social effort should be directed to keeping families together at all costs. The decision to remove the child from his home is absolutely the last resort. "Underlying the provisions of the Children Act (of 1948) is the conviction that family life is the most important experience that any child can have, and the aim of the service which the Act establishes is to preserve, restore, or create family life for children in whose circumstances it is threatened."[2]

Sir Jocelyn Simon, President of the High Court's Probate, Divorce and Admiralty Division, said in June, 1965: "It is sometimes argued that a home broken by divorce is better for a child than a home where the parents are deeply at odds. But it is by no means an infrequent experience of judges sitting in custody jurisdiction that it is at the moment of the break-up of the home that one finds a sudden and alarming deterioration in the child —bad behaviour, speech disorders, plummeting down in class."

Even the months of prior squabbling, Sir Jocelyn maintained, affected the child less than the break-up of the family. So he argued that no divorce should be allowed for parents with children aged up to 16 or 17. Whether we agree with this or not as a practical legal measure the following statement of his is worth noting: "We have got ourselves into a position where we are spending annually, through legal aid, £4 million on promoting the break-up of marriages. This is about one hundred times more than the sum which, through marriage guidance and education, we are spending to promote the endurance of marriages."

This, if anything, is a sign of the inability of man to use his reason well. If marriage is the basic structure of society, all our efforts financial and otherwise should be directed towards

---

[1] *Ibid.*, p. 170.   [2] *Ibid.*, p. 174.

keeping the family secure. Much more marriage and family counselling needs to be undertaken by qualified personnel, especially in regard to sex-guidance and child-welfare.

It is incredible that sex should still be regarded in some quarters as something purely instinctual, the offices of which do not have to be taught. Apart from the techniques of sex, the idea that sexuality should be the expression of the whole affective life and the tender emotions is unknown to many. And if the doctors are to be believed the number of women who pass the whole of their married lives without satisfaction, simply because the husband has no notion of the differences in physiological reaction between the sexes, is astonishing.

In parenthesis, I should say that what is often the saddest element in pre-marital sex is that it is used as a substitute for love and tender emotion instead of becoming their fulfilment or perfect expression in marriage, when self-dedication to another has been consecrated and made final. Before marriage sexual experience is too likely to be a frenzied, guilty and biological (or animal) thing. A pure courtship refines sexuality, so that sexuality is more completely human, more spiritual—which does not mean it is less pleasurable. Rather the exact opposite is the case. After such a pure courtship it is exceedingly clear that *sex* cannot be equated with biological faculties but is a matter of the whole orientation of one's individual being, biological, psychical, spiritual, to another. The act of sex can then become the expression of the whole personality and not only of an unspiritualized part of it. In such circumstances love will last.

Unhappy sexual adjustment in marriage is often no doubt due to a too early experience of the purely physiological side of sex. That experience gives a false or, at best, very superficial notion of what is to be demanded, and what can be expected in a relationship between the sexes.

Such misunderstanding is liable to lead to infidelity, the eventual break-up of the family and the production of neurotic children who, when they grow up, will produce neurotic children in their turn. An intense form of child and family guidance is necessary to counter the forces making for the dissolution of the family. Foremost among these forces is ignorance.

The teen-age problem

The data provided by child psychologists also enable us to have insights into what is called the teen-age problem. Firstly, we should note that there is no such thing as a teen-age problem in isolation from infant, adult and parental problems. Obviously adolescents have difficulties to cope with which are specific to them, the conscious awakening of sex, the need of emotional independence, a measure of freedom whereby they can exert their adulthood and autonomy but not so much that they feel completely lost and helpless and inevitably disillusioned with life. These are difficulties and genuine enough: they only become "problems" in the social sense when the adolescents have not the means to deal with them adequately. This is most often because parents for some reason or other have not been able to provide these means. The troublesome adolescent is usually the deprived child who has simply grown up. He is anti-social only because he never experienced over a period, when a child, the love which is the cohesive force in all social relationships.

It is very sad when intelligent people are still reluctant to accept this well-based fact. Whenever there is an outbreak of adolescent disturbances there is irresponsible talk about bringing back the "cat" and the stocks and so on. The newspapers fly the headline "Battle of Hastings"; even magistrates use verbally aggressive phrases like "sawdust Caesars". Such an eye-for-an-eye attitude is neither Christian nor humane. Punishment administered with the least semblance of vindictiveness by people for whom they have no respect, with no cognizance being taken of the emotional void in which they live, cannot but harm teenagers further and so the society of which they are a part. Punishment, it is true, is for the most part necessary and salutary. But to punish these offenders without sympathy is to convince them that society's opposition to and separation from them is now complete.

It may seem idealistic to say that disturbed adolescents can only be cured by understanding and love. It so happens that society, as experience shows, has no alternative to the idealistic. Nothing else works.

Such research as has been done indicates that most boys who go to Borstal are not effectively helped to become more adaptable, social human beings. Little successful assistance is offered to cure their emotional disorders. They remain, as a consequence, in the words of one psychiatrist, part of that 10 per cent who use 90 per cent of the social services.[1] New methods need to be devised to regain them for society, and new small institutional forms experimented with, after the pattern of family and home life.

Anybody who has read the deplorable history of the treatment of mental illnesses will appreciate how the advances in psychiatric medicine have meant not only an advance in the knowledge of human nature but also a growth in pity. Since men are social beings, their sociability can be made or marred in their earliest years in their family environment. We are exploring more fully than before the social factors which help make a person the kind of person he is. An adolescent brought up without any love at all cannot be expected to grow into a particularly sociable person; nor are we likely to make him more lovable by beating him. So much is the personality formed in the earliest years of infancy that often much later a sudden, otherwise unaccountable change in the behaviour of a normal adult can be explained by something that happened to him many years earlier and which he may have forgotten or never known.

It is curious, as I remarked, how much opposition is aroused

[1] D. Miller, *Growth to Freedom*, op. cit., p. 100.

to the findings of psychiatric medicine by men with axes to grind. For example, the philosopher might say: "If you accept the theory that infancy can have lasting effects on a person's character and actions, what becomes of freedom?" The moral theologian may not want to enlarge the field of mental illness too much because that would diminish the field of sin, and no one likes to feel on his cheek the warm sour breath of redundancy. The die-hard brought up in Victorian days when children were expected to be seen and not heard is liable to become all biblical, "Spare the rod and spoil the child." Opposition on all scores is due to misunderstanding. The intention is not to deny sin but to re-map its territory—and to indicate that sin is often much more in the situation than in the individual. Christians above all are theologically prepared to accept the social character of sin, sin in its collective aspect, what scripture calls "the sin of the world". *This* is the primary affront to God which Christ came to take upon himself. Perhaps some axes have to be ground for generation after generation until there is nothing left, and well-meaning prejudice can be replaced by reason.

Once more the consideration of unmanageable and delinquent children demonstrates that from the point of view of sheer economy money spent on family guidance is money well-spent. For every child in a public home and for every delinquent in a penal institution the State has to pay out something over £500 per year. From the inveterate criminal there are no compensatings returns at all. To build up an elaborate penal system and to be niggardly in the expenditure on family and marriage guidance is really to show that reason, even in the learned, sometimes has a ring through its nose.

Of course there is in existence already a whole body of social case-workers labouring tirelessly and selflessly for the good of the community—probation officers, child-care officers, psychiatric social workers, almoners and so on. But their number needs to be augmented. Perhaps the advent of automation will make this possible, though, if the truth be told, it will probably make it even more necessary than it is now. I can even foresee the title of a sociological book of the future, "Suicide and Cybernetics".

Conclusion

Enough has been said to show that reflection on the primary importance of the family to society indicates the need to strengthen our social services, not to supplant the family but to support it, to make the family members more adequate to solve their own problems and so to achieve a wider measure of independence.

We need more emphasis in the universities on social work, more comprehensive and flexible youth services, more family advice and counselling centres. We need additional vocational training centres to help the family become more self-supporting and self-respecting. We must strengthen by all the resources at our disposal the links between the family and the school; and one way of doing this is to make the teaching profession a better-paid and more honourable profession than politicians are inclined to make it. Money and dedication are not necessarily unhappy bed-fellows. In fact, if there were better financial rewards for teaching there would be a more adequate supply of teachers. The result would be that the really dedicated ones among them could engage in true creative work rather than be condemned to spending most of their time and energy in enforcing discipline upon an overcrowded class of children. We must see that our homes and institutions are imaginative and staffed with well-qualified personnel so that they are not antechambers to Borstal. And if I may add one further suggestion it is that women should be encouraged to take a more pronounced part in social life to help us truly understand the matters of which I have been but airily speaking.

I have said nothing about the role of the Church in these

matters. I have not mentioned except *en passant* the sacrament of matrimony which fashions the family after the likeness of Christ and his bride, the Church, which is ever fruitful of children. I have made no reference to the problems of family limitation.

I wanted to show on just how broad an empirical basis rests the Church's constant teaching on the sacredness of family life and the indissolubility of marriage, especially when there are children involved. A study of the social and psychological sciences in particular vindicates the Church's long and heroic struggle to safeguard the institution of the family, one of whose principal aims is "the preservation of the art of parenthood".